Cute Animal Coloring Book for Kids

Illustrations by Gaurav S

Dedicated to all the young artists who bring color to the world. May your creativity shine brightly!

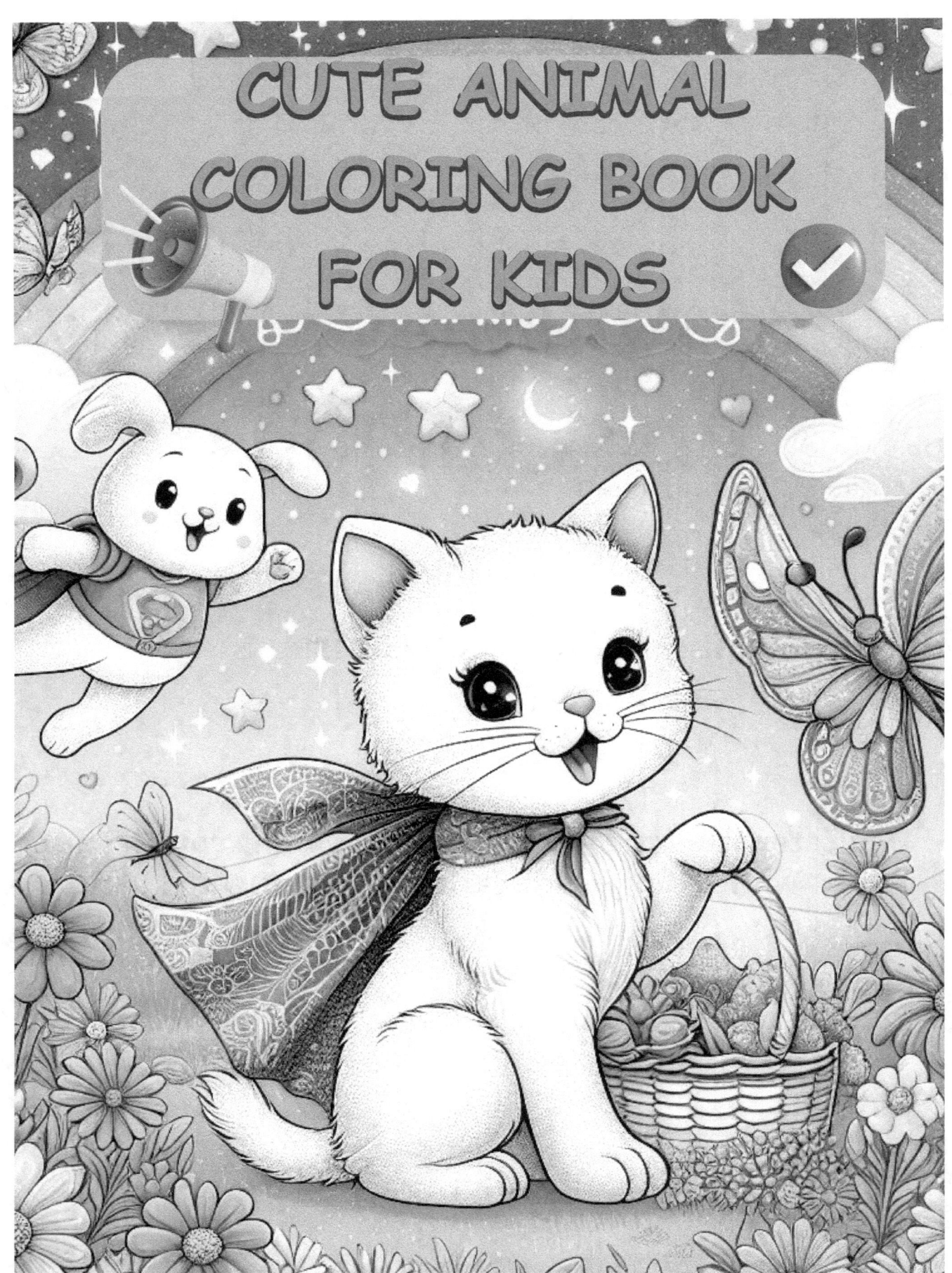

Introduction

Welcome to the Cute Animal Coloring Book for Kids!

Get ready to embark on a magical journey filled with adorable animals and enchanting scenes. Each page of this book is designed to spark your imagination and creativity. Whether it's a playful kitten chasing a butterfly or a superhero puppy saving the day, you'll find plenty of delightful pictures to color and enjoy.

This coloring book features beautiful illustrations by **Gaurav S**., whose art brings each animal and scene to life. We hope you have as much fun coloring these pages as we did creating them.

Grab your favorite coloring tools and let the adventure begin!

Happy coloring!

Index

1. Kitten Chasing a Butterfly ------------------------- Page 7-18
2. Superhero Puppy ------------------------------------ Page 19-26
3. Bunnies Having a Picnic ---------------------------- Page 27-34
4. Baby Elephant Splashing in a Pond ----------------- Page 35-46
5. Kitten and Puppy Snuggled in a Basket ------------ Page 47-54
6. Bunnies in a Vegetable Garden --------------------- Page 55-62
7. Baby Elephants Playing with a Ball ---------------- Page 63-70
8. Cats and Dogs at the Beach ------------------------ Page 71-76
9. Cat in Space -------------------------------------- Page 77-84
10. Dog Circus --------------------------------------- Page 85-92
11. Bunnies in Winter -------------------------------- Page 93-100
12. Elephants in a Jungle ---------------------------- Page 101-106

Special thanks to **Gaurav S**. for the incredible illustrations that make this book truly magical.

How to Use This Book

1. Choose Your Colors: Pick your favorite crayons, colored pencils, or markers. The possibilities are endless!

2. Start Coloring: Each page is printed on single-sided paper to prevent colors from bleeding through. Feel free to remove pages to share with friends and family.

3. Get Creative: Don't be afraid to use different colors and techniques. This is your book, and you can make each picture as unique as you are.

4. Display Your Art: Once you've finished a page, consider displaying your masterpiece on the fridge or in your room.

Remember, there's no right or wrong way to color. The most important thing is to have fun and let your creativity soar!

About the Illustrator

Gaurav S. is an artist known for creating charming and whimsical illustrations that captivate children and adults alike. With a passion for bringing stories to life through art, Gaurav's work in this coloring book is sure to inspire young artists to explore their creativity.

Thank you for choosing this book. Happy coloring!

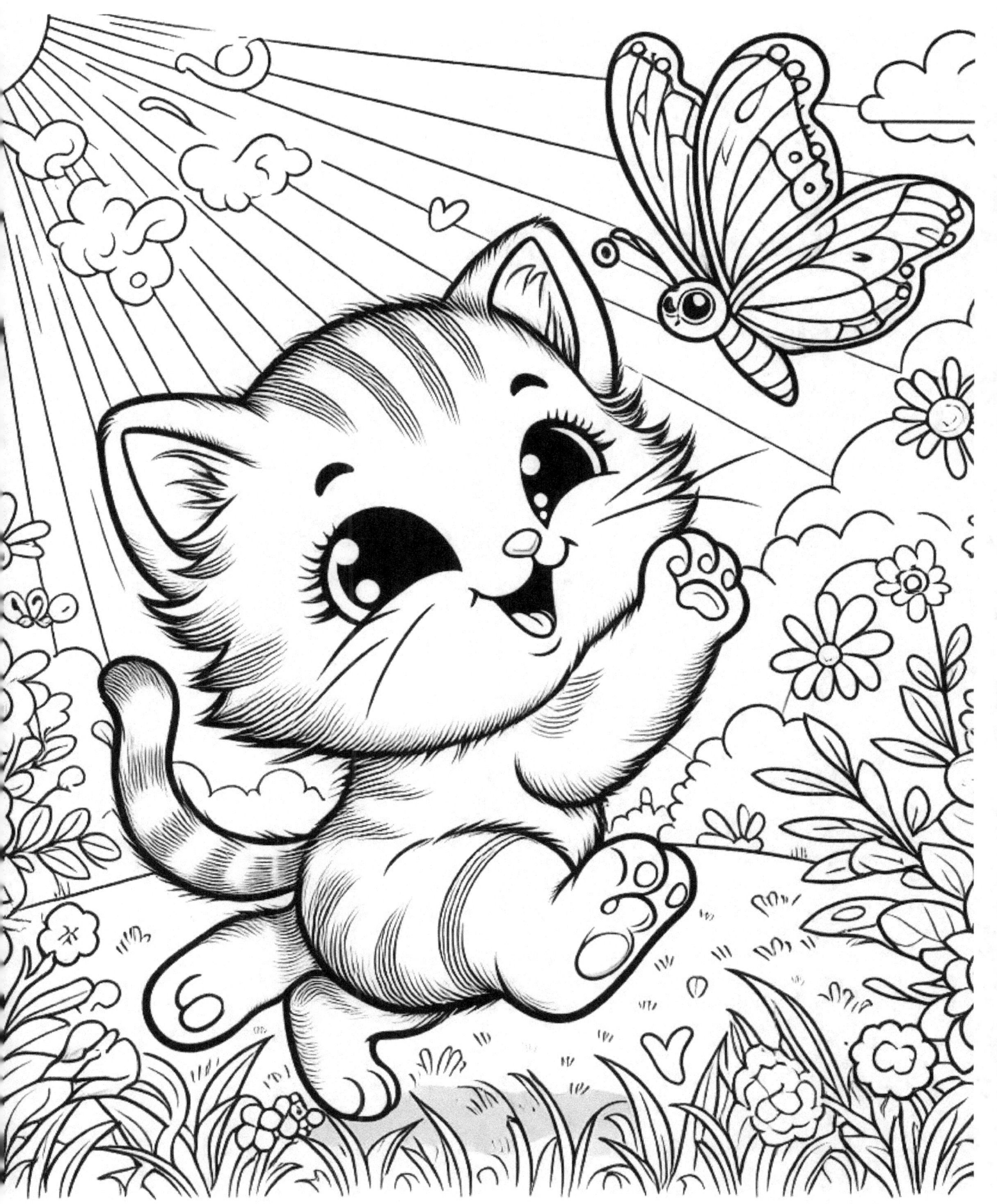

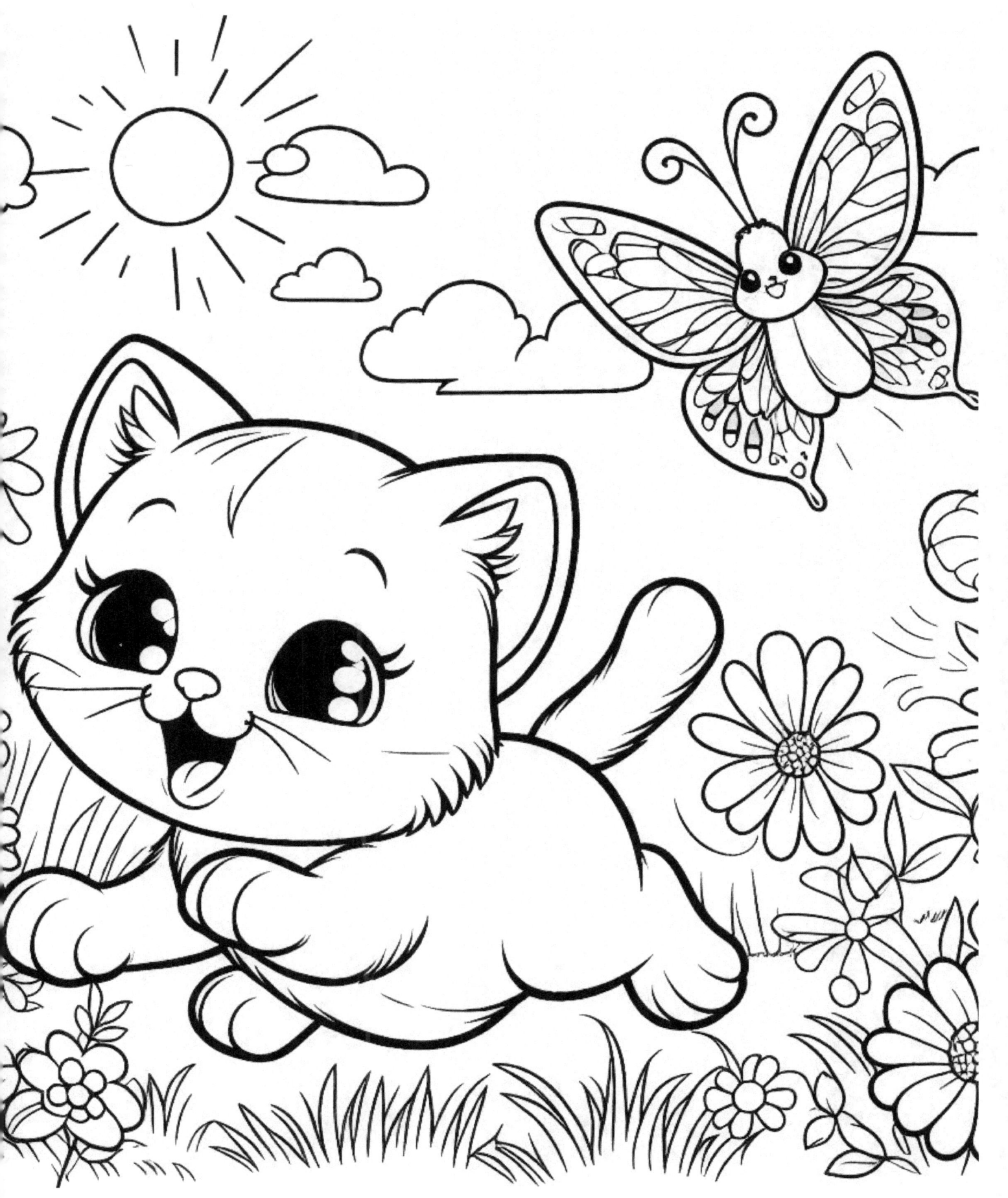

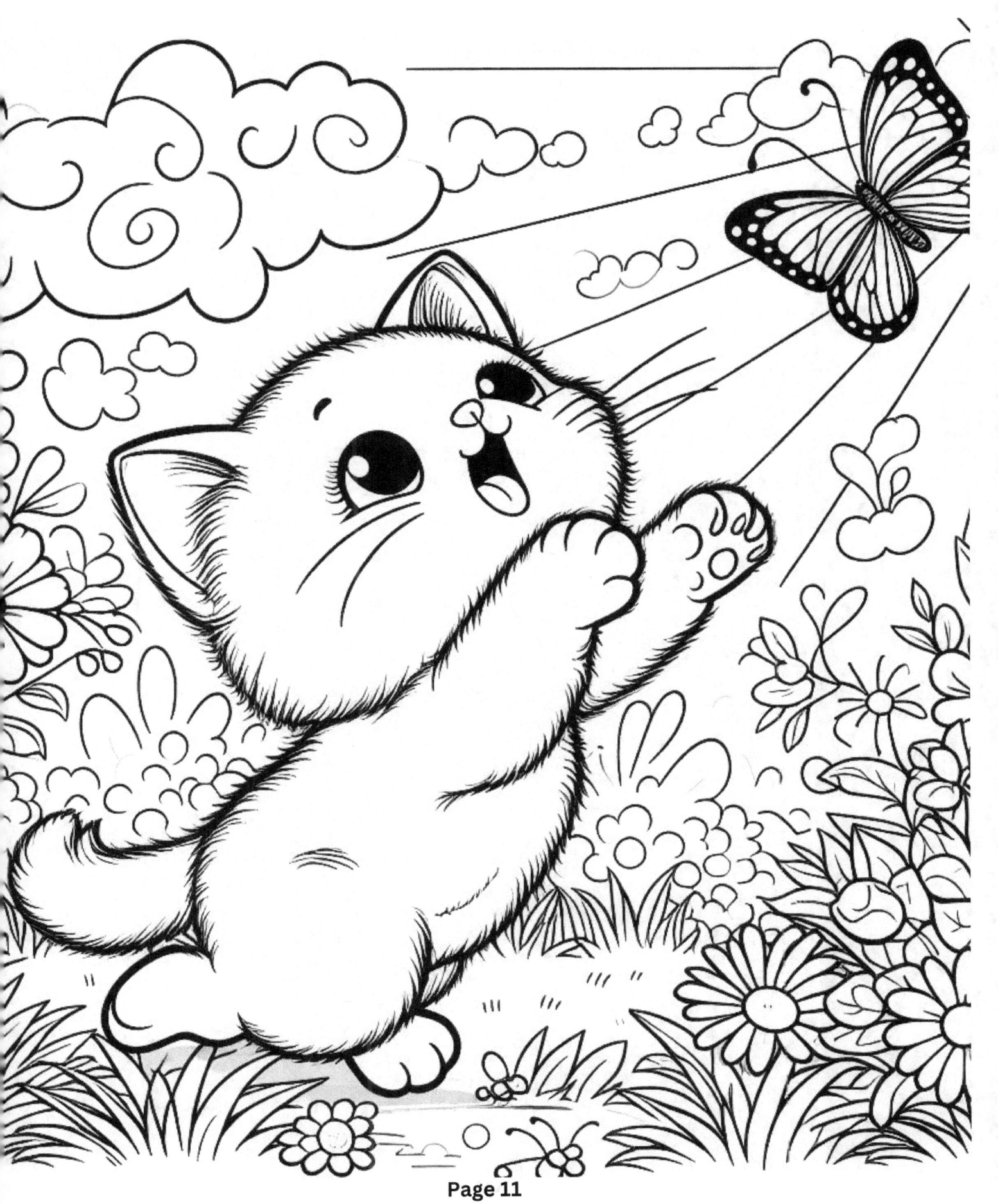

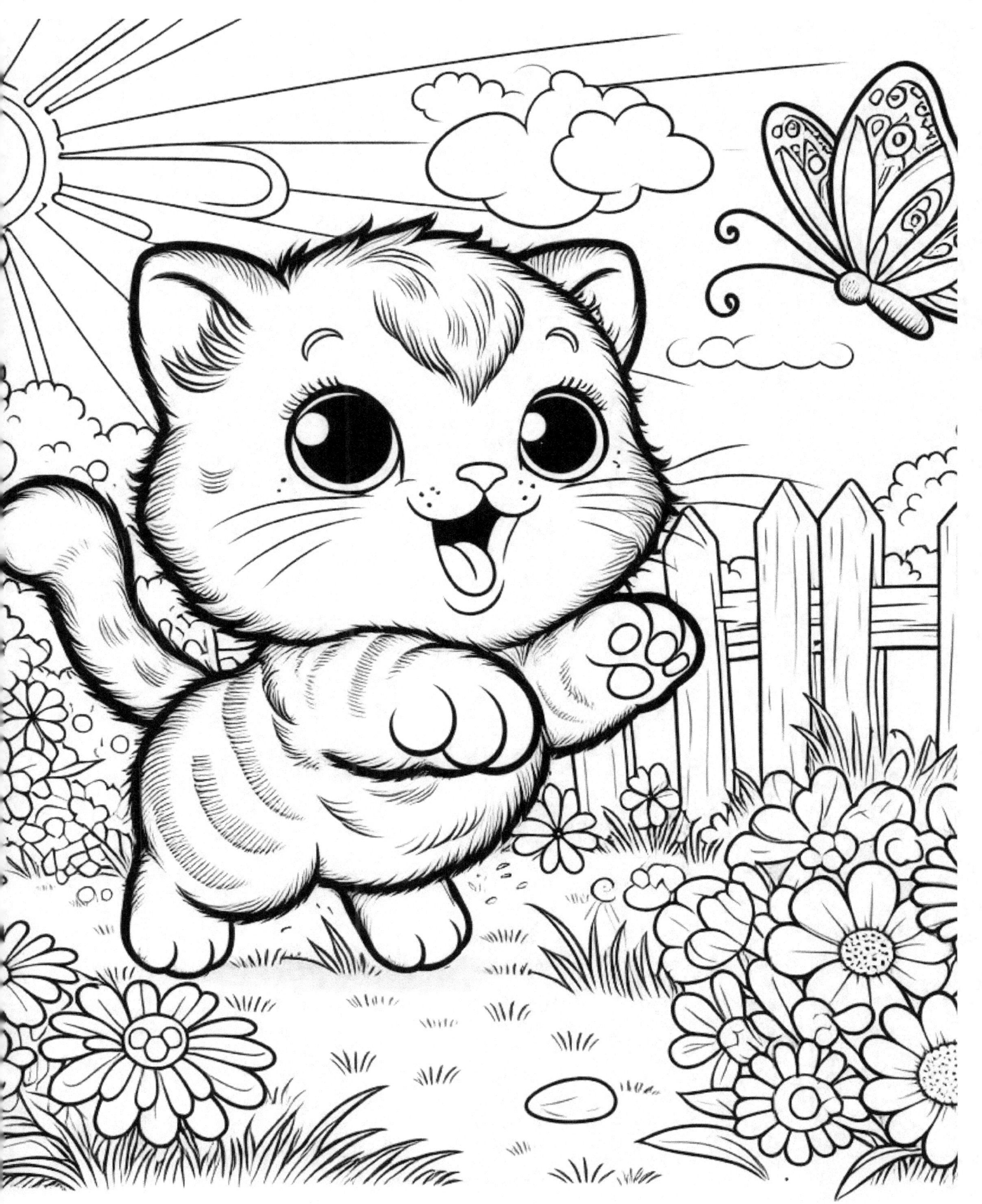

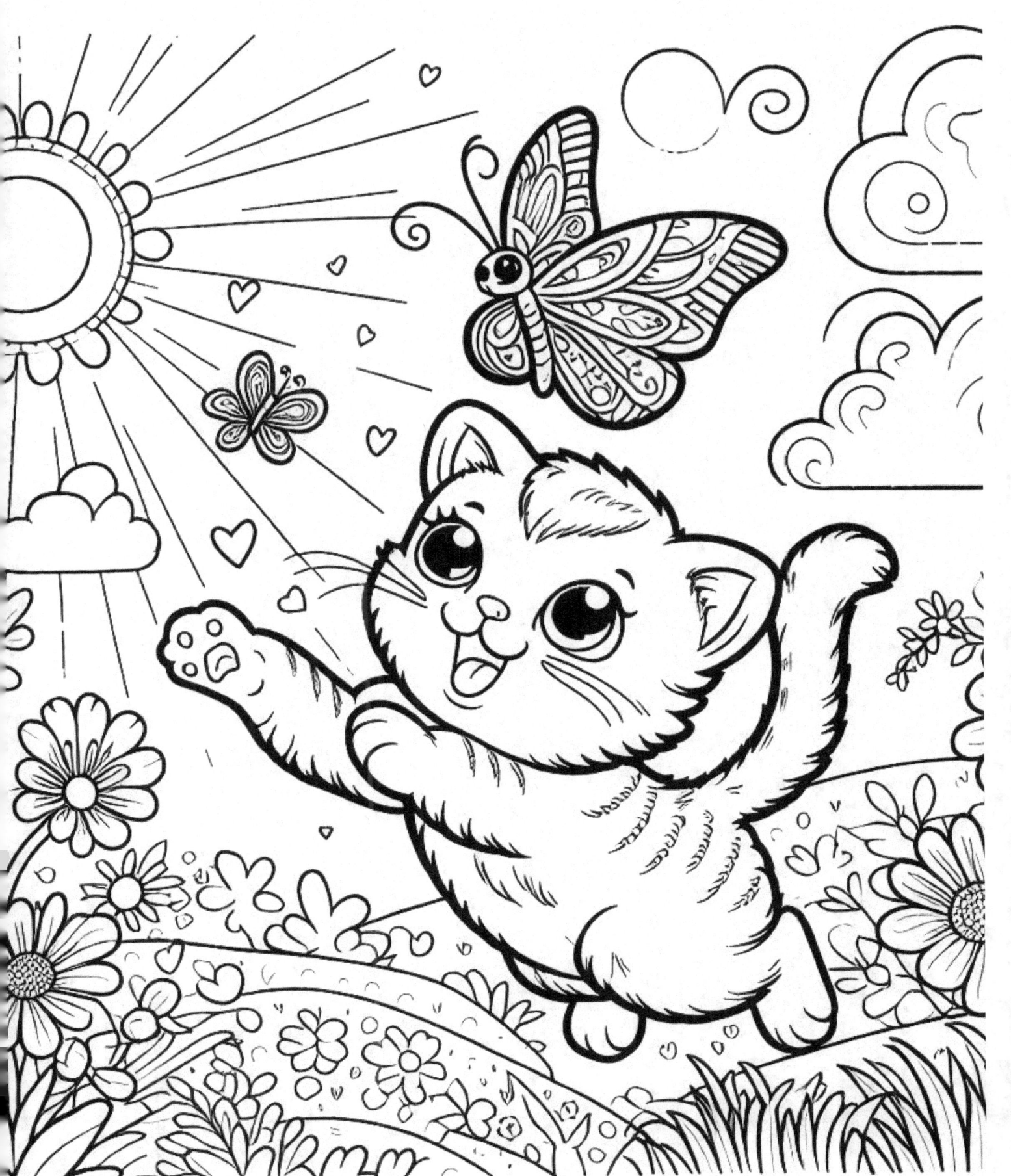

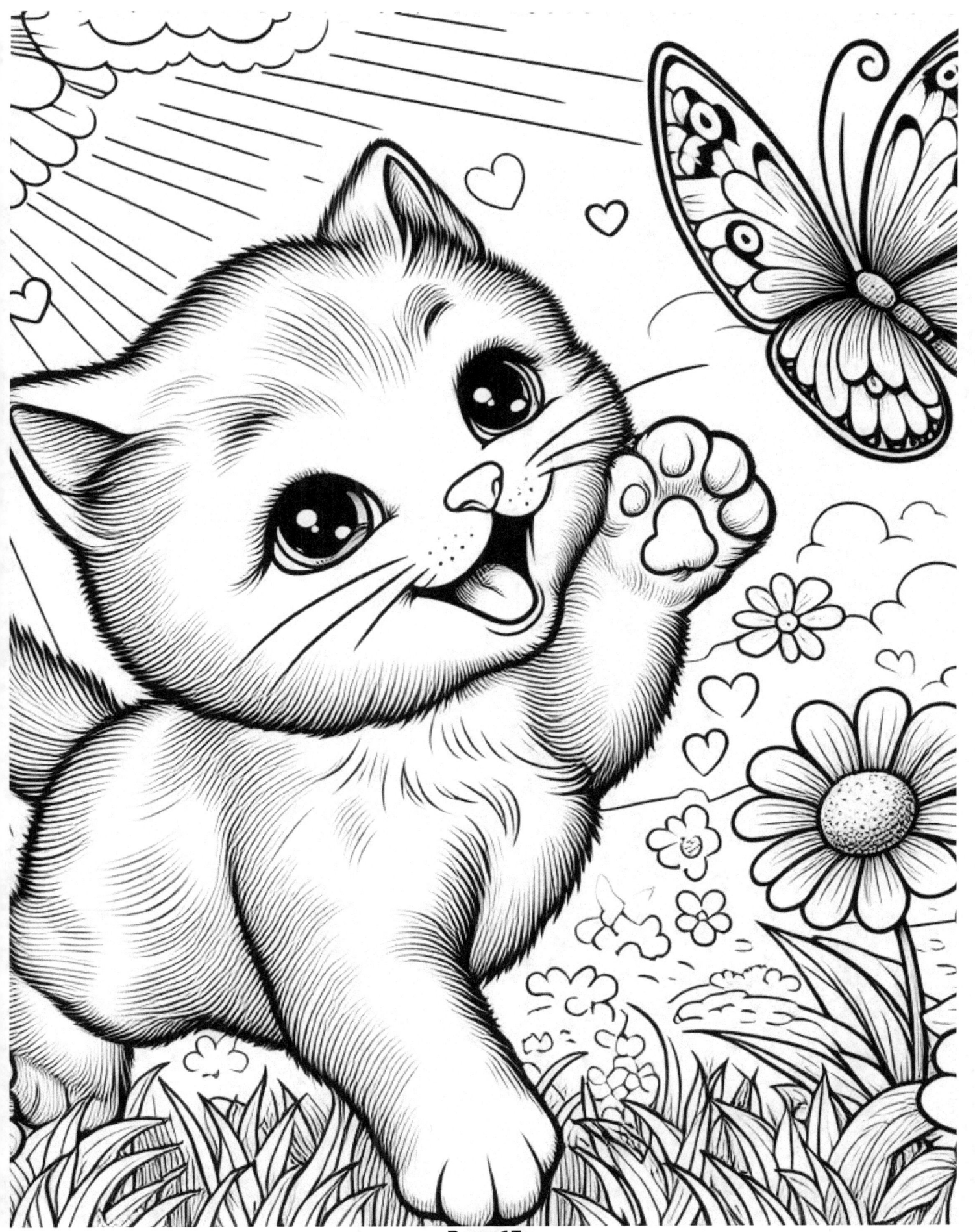

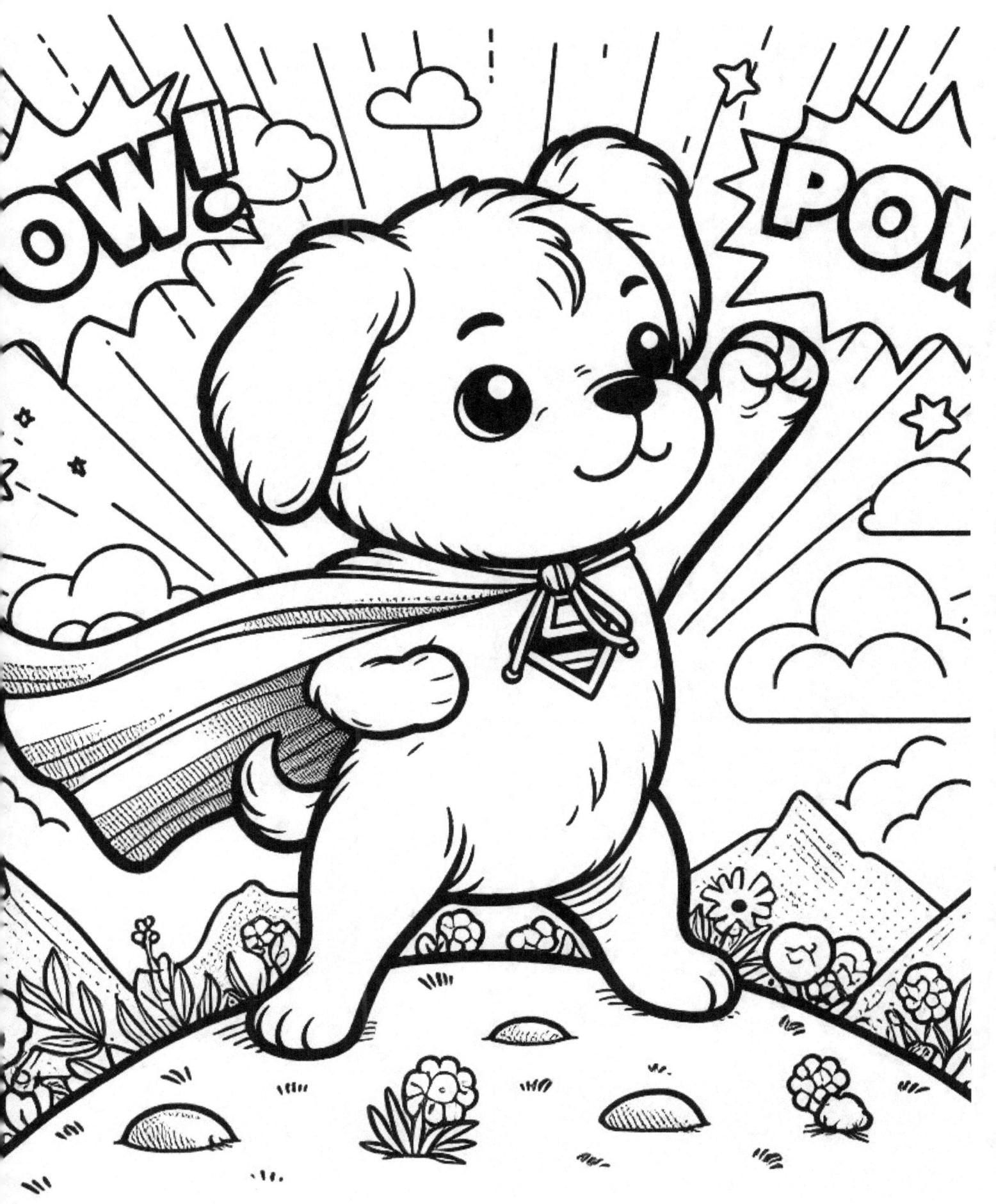

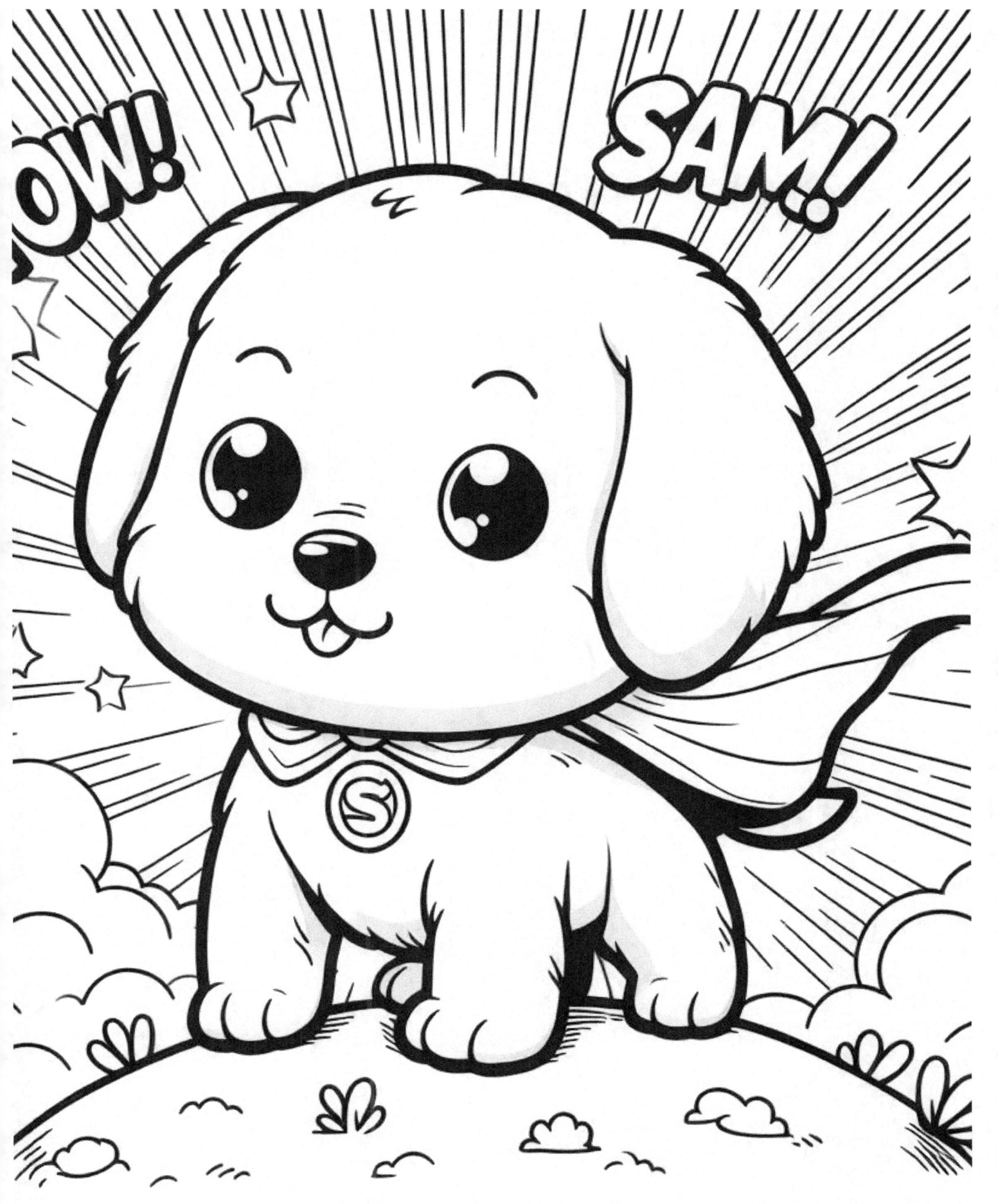

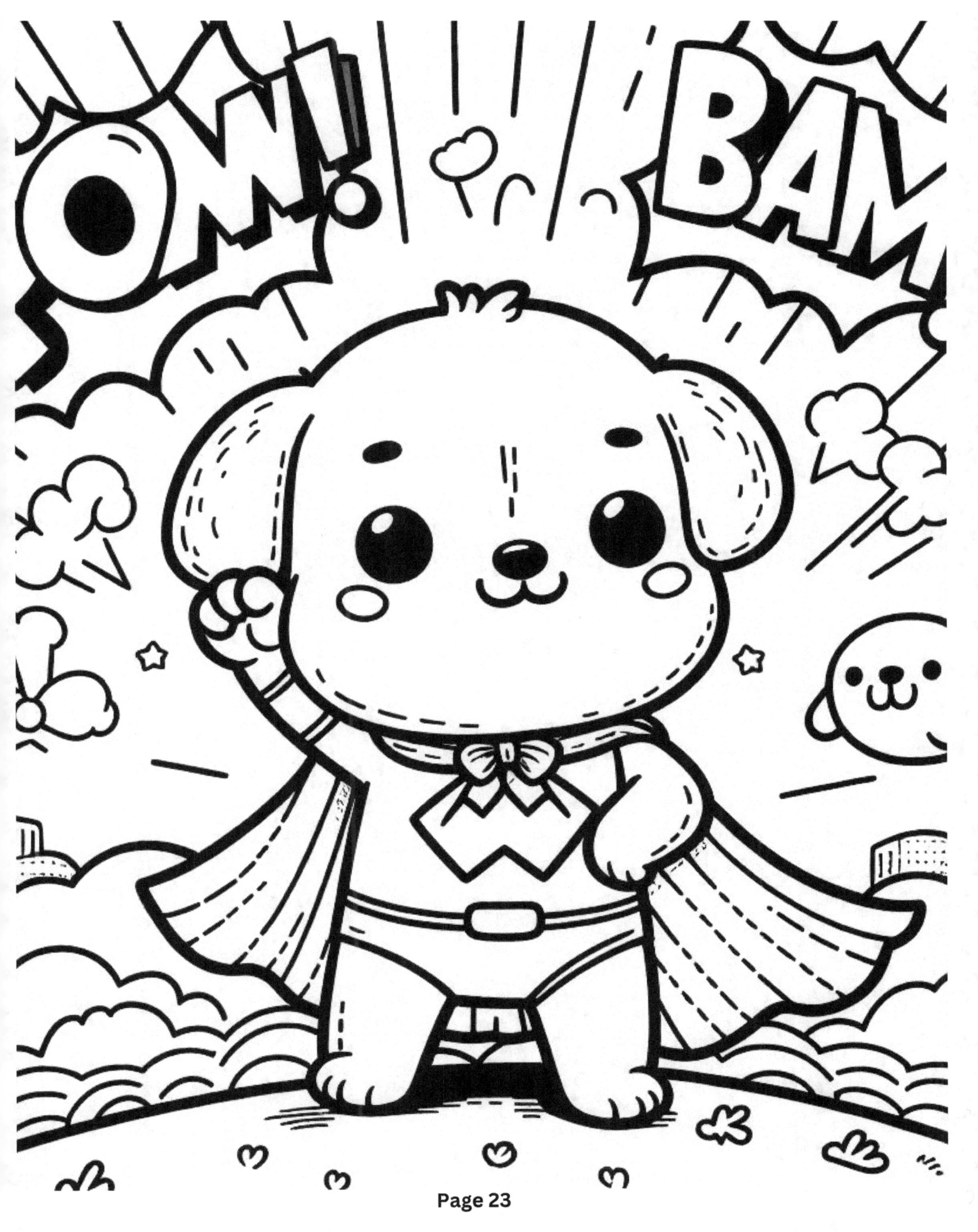

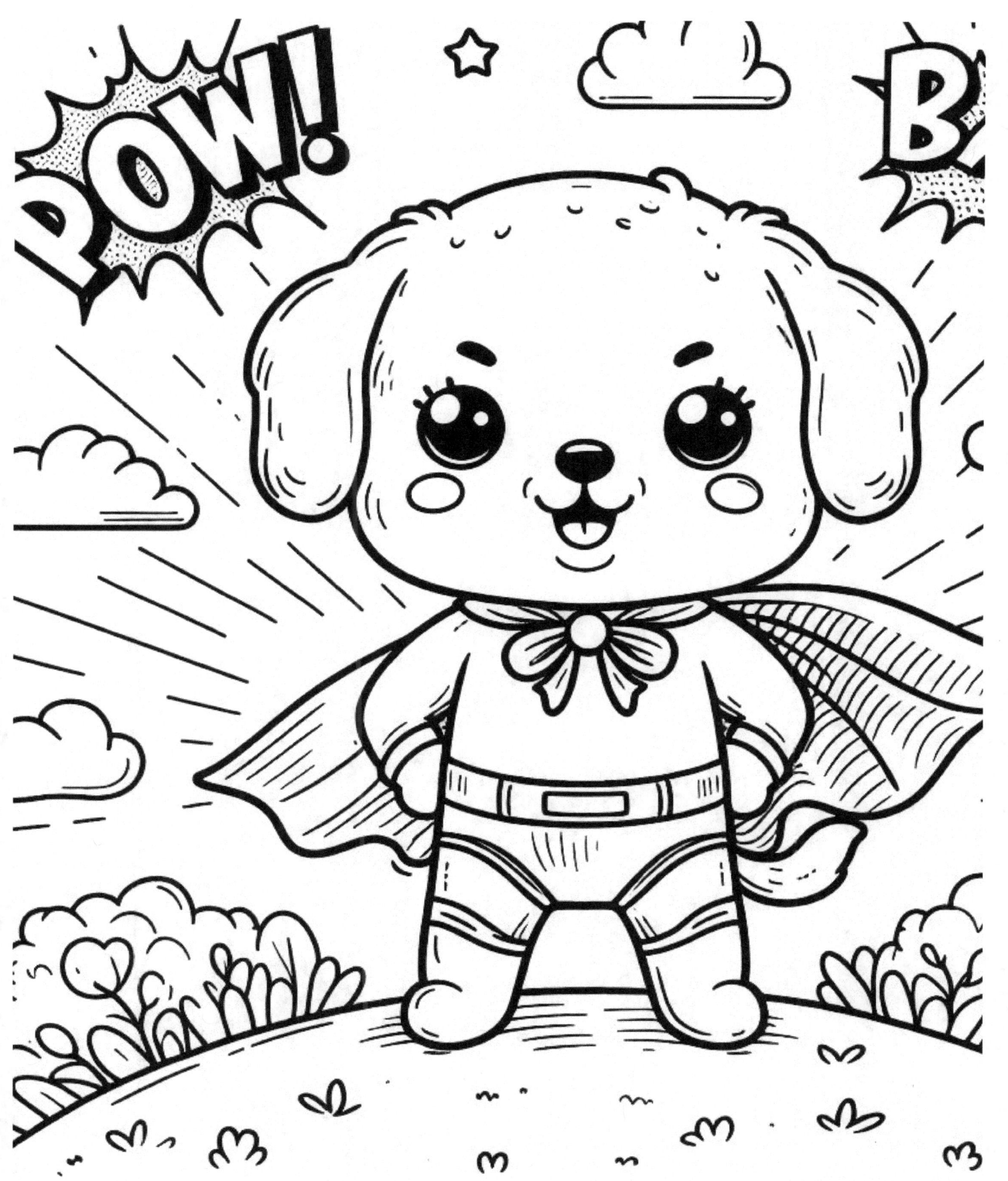

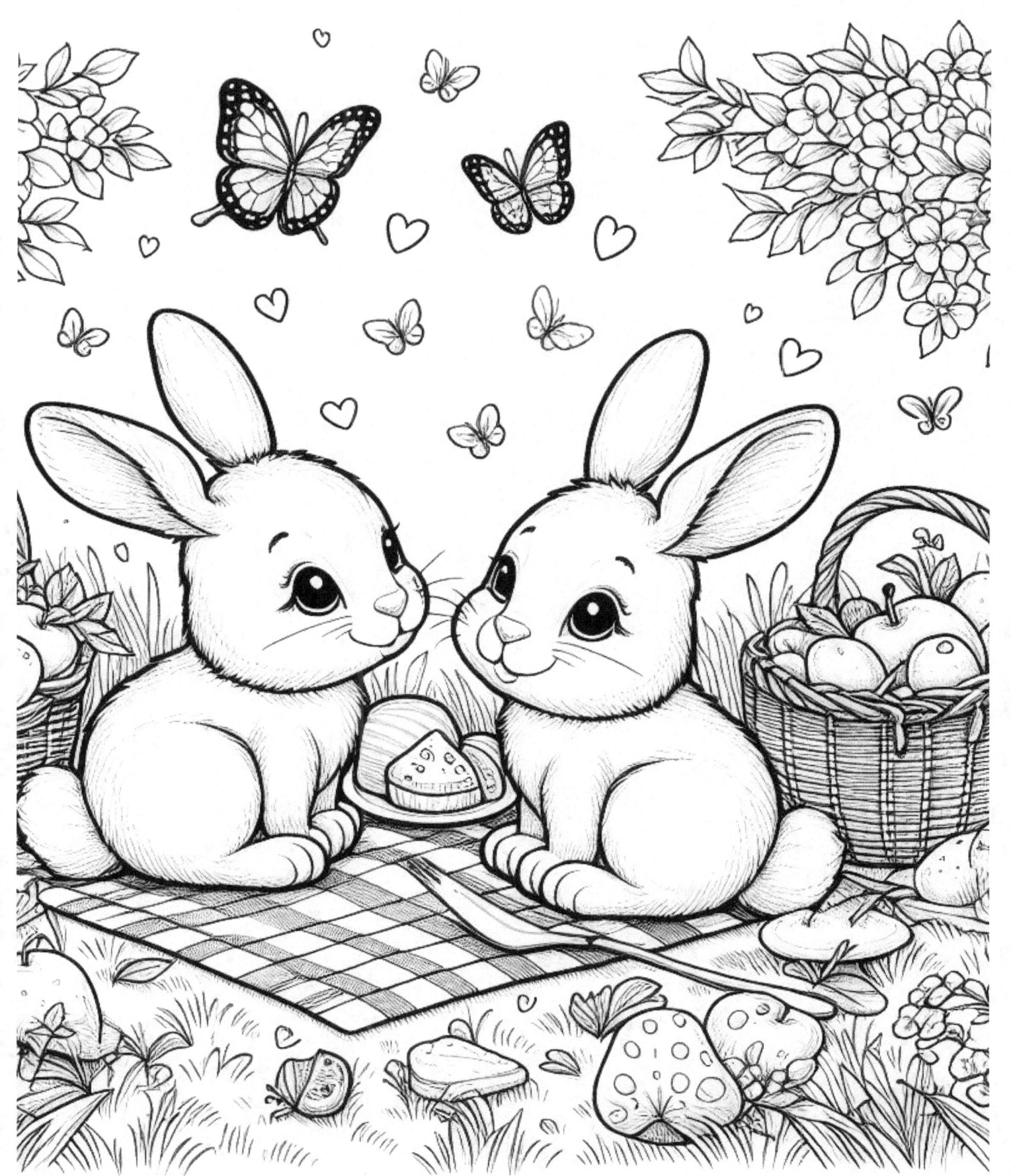

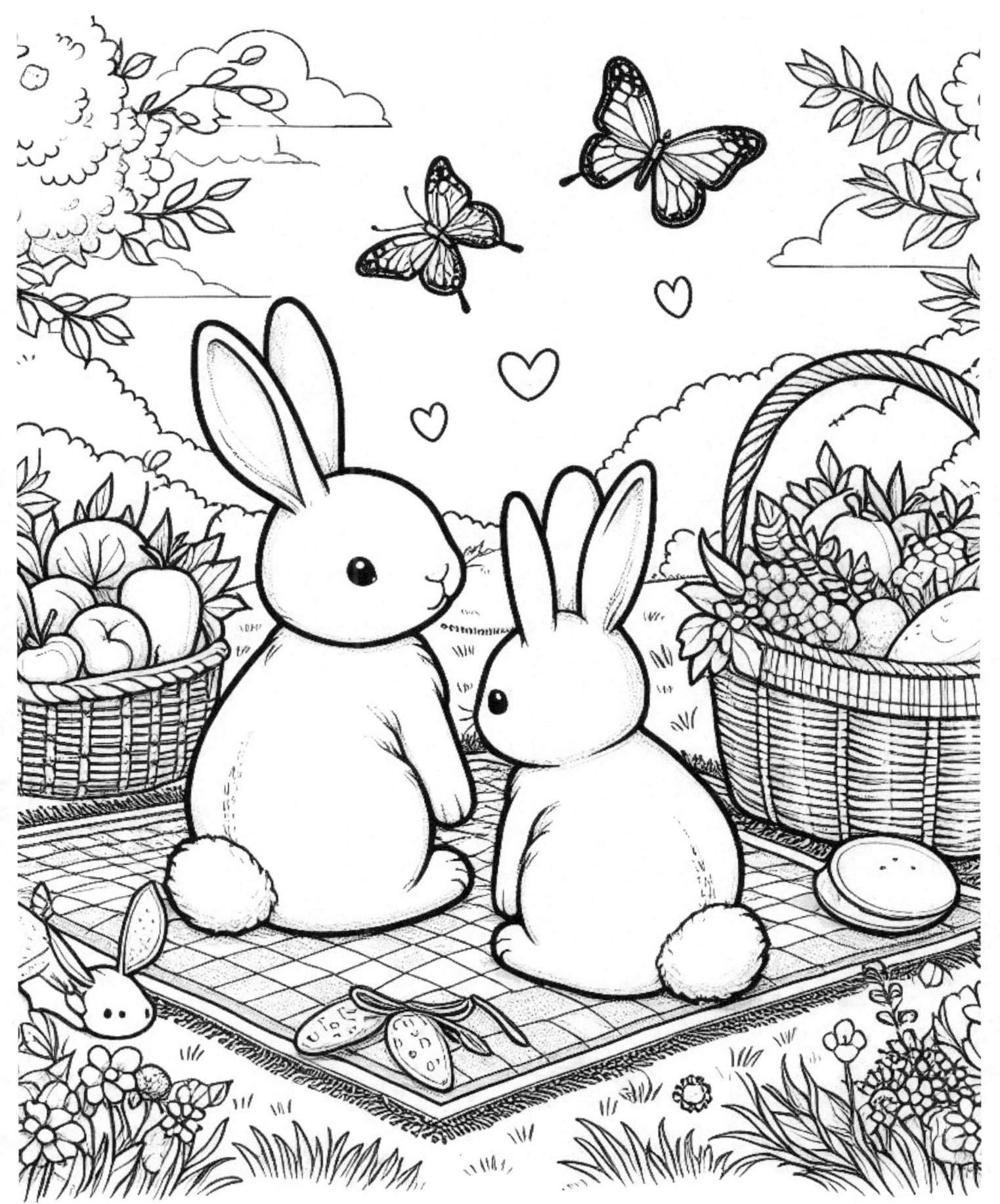

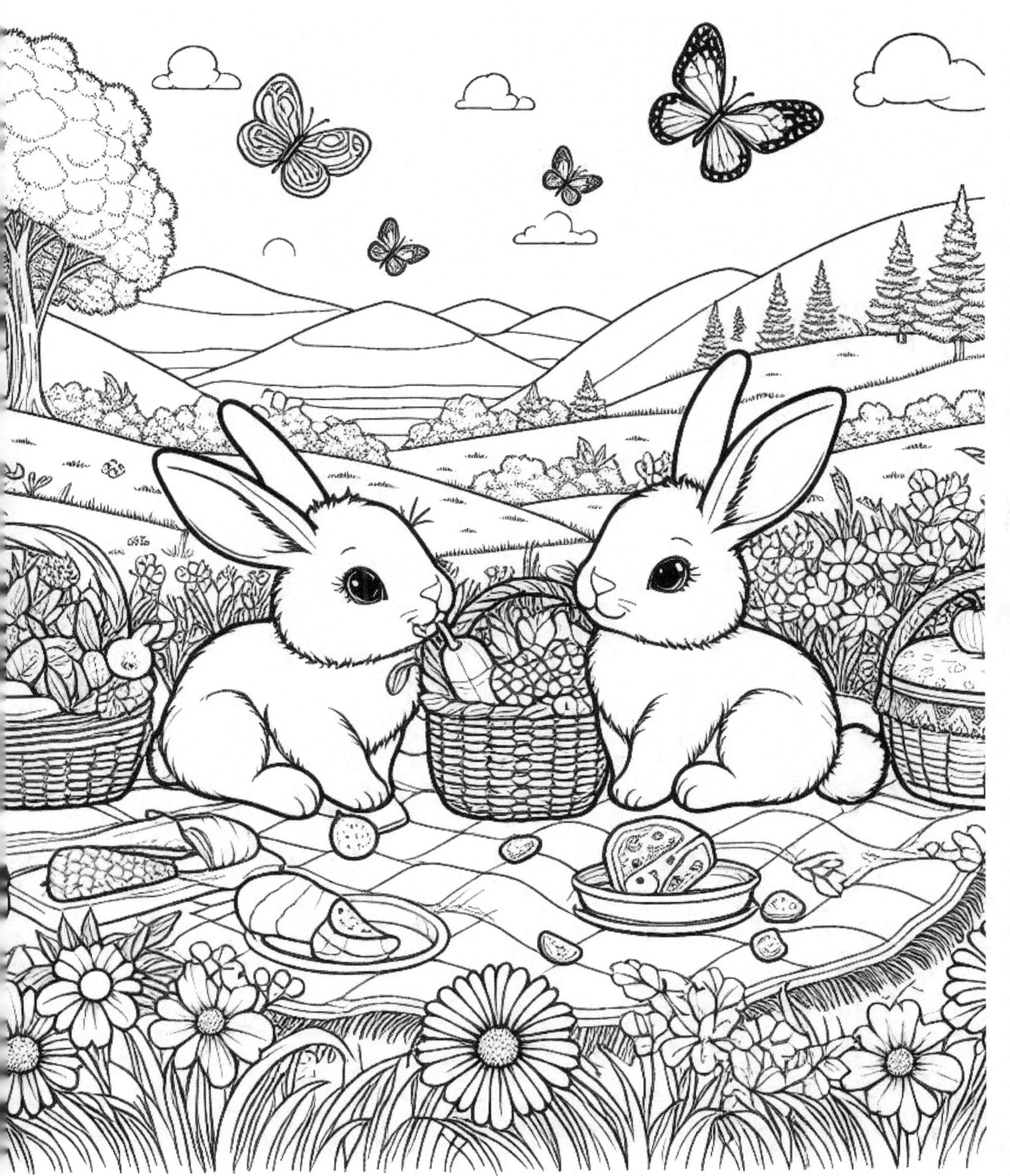

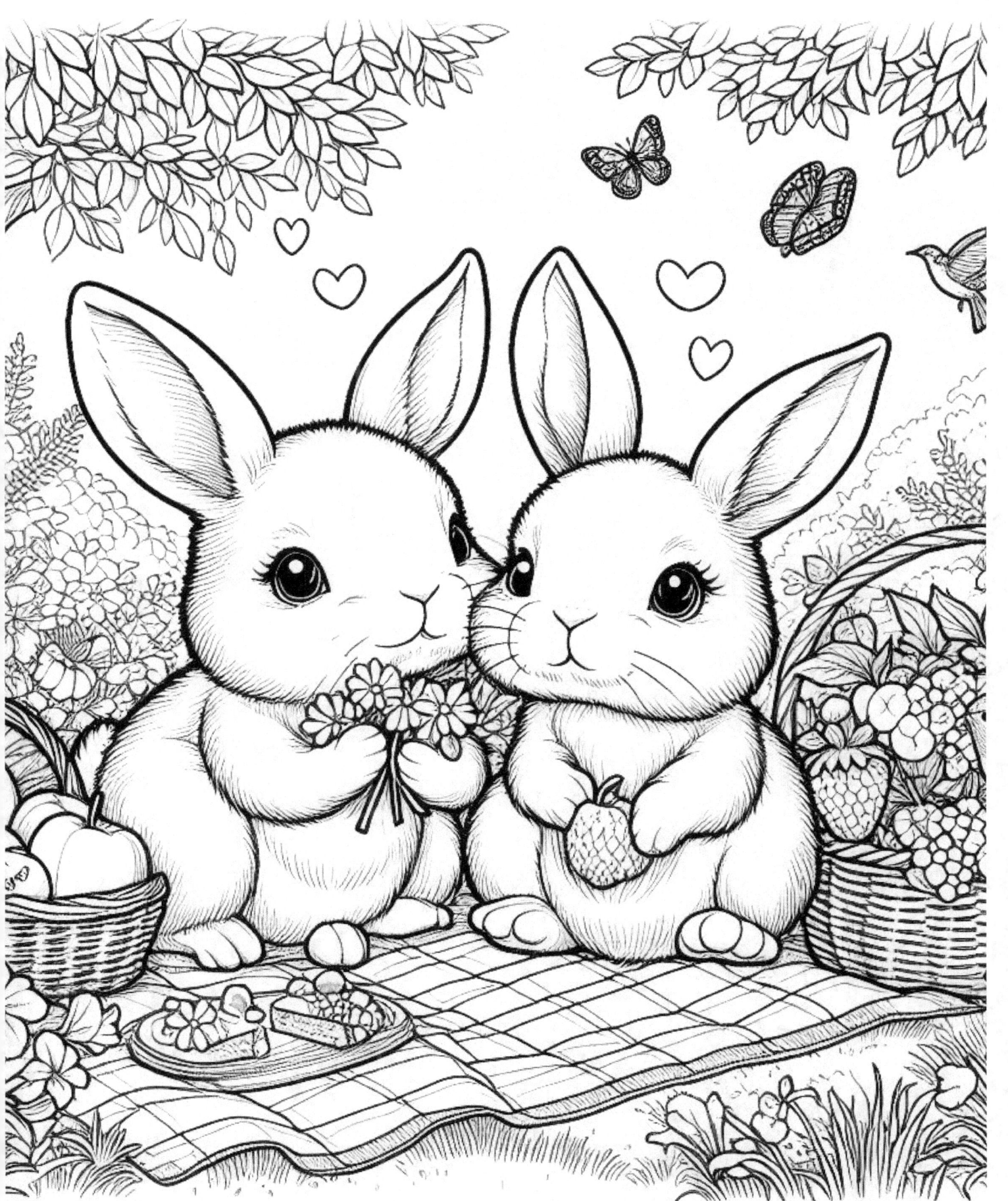

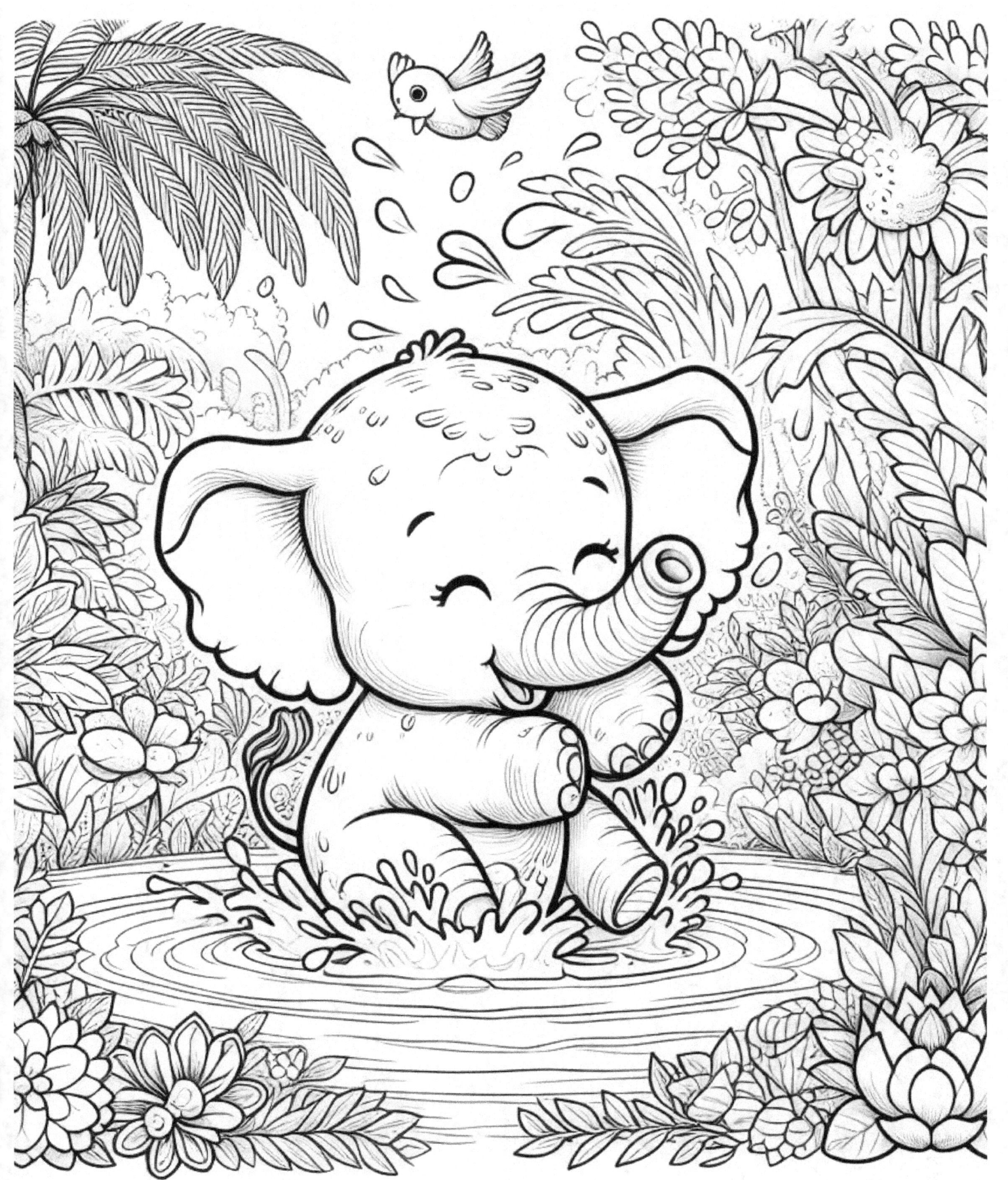

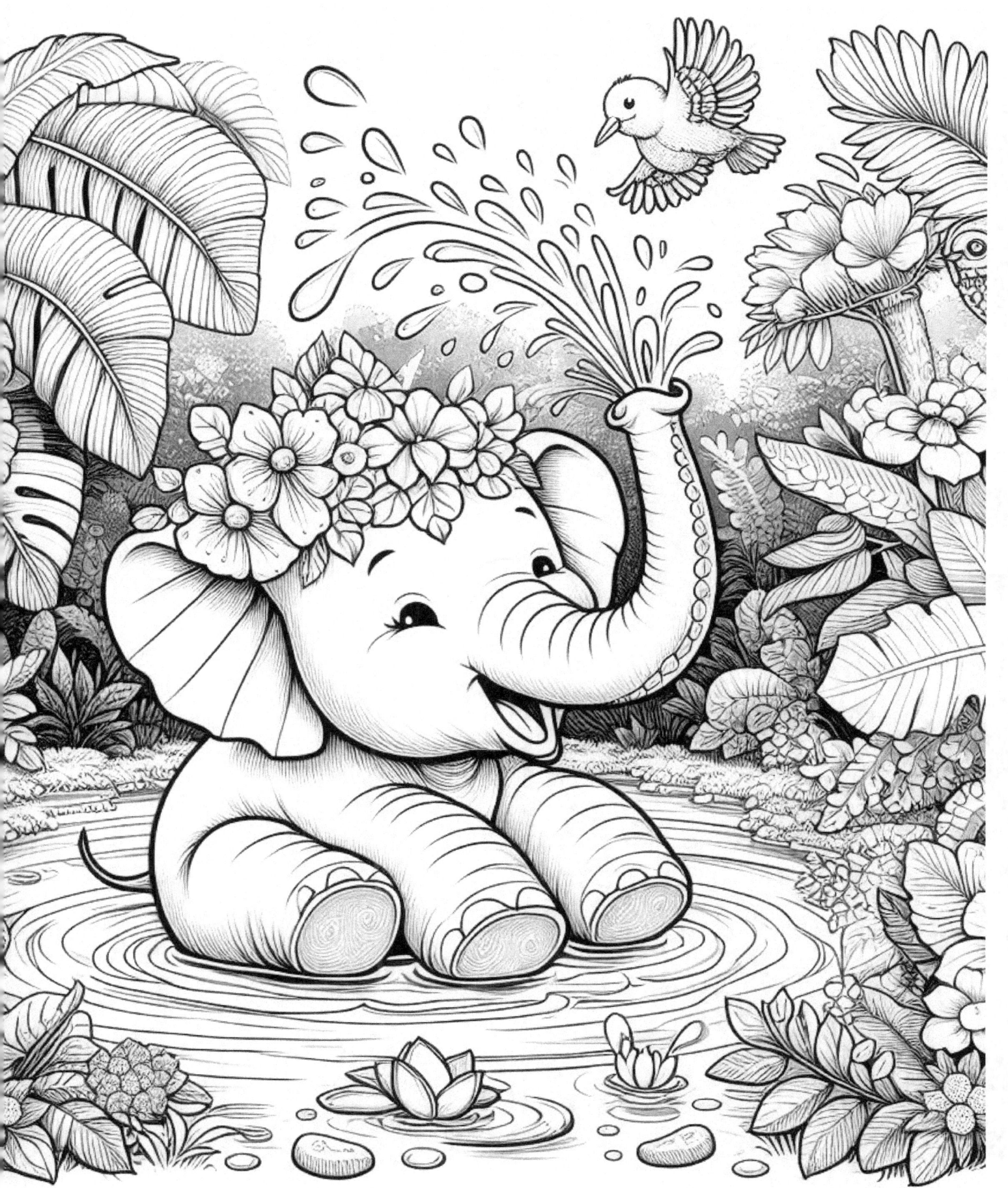

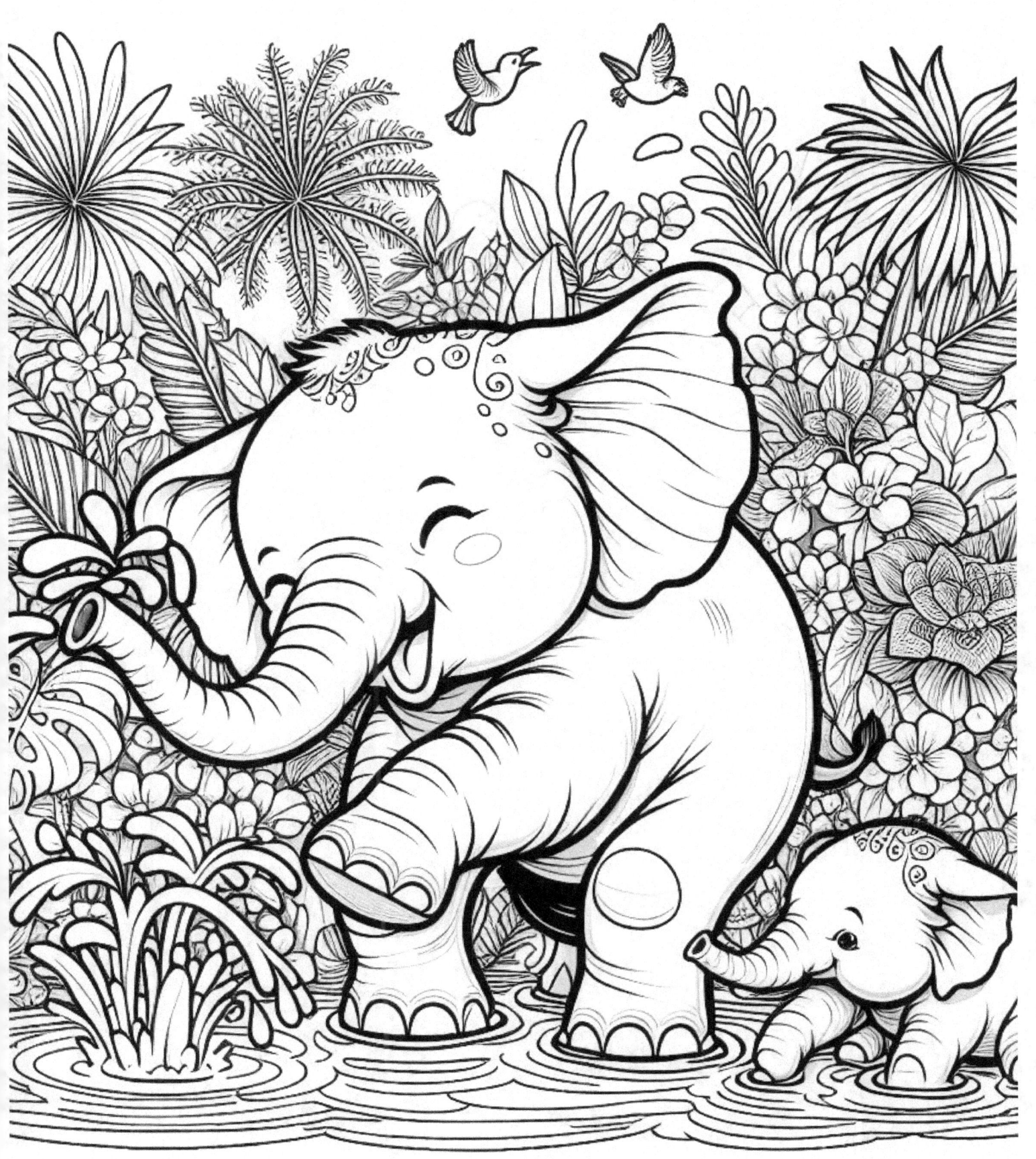

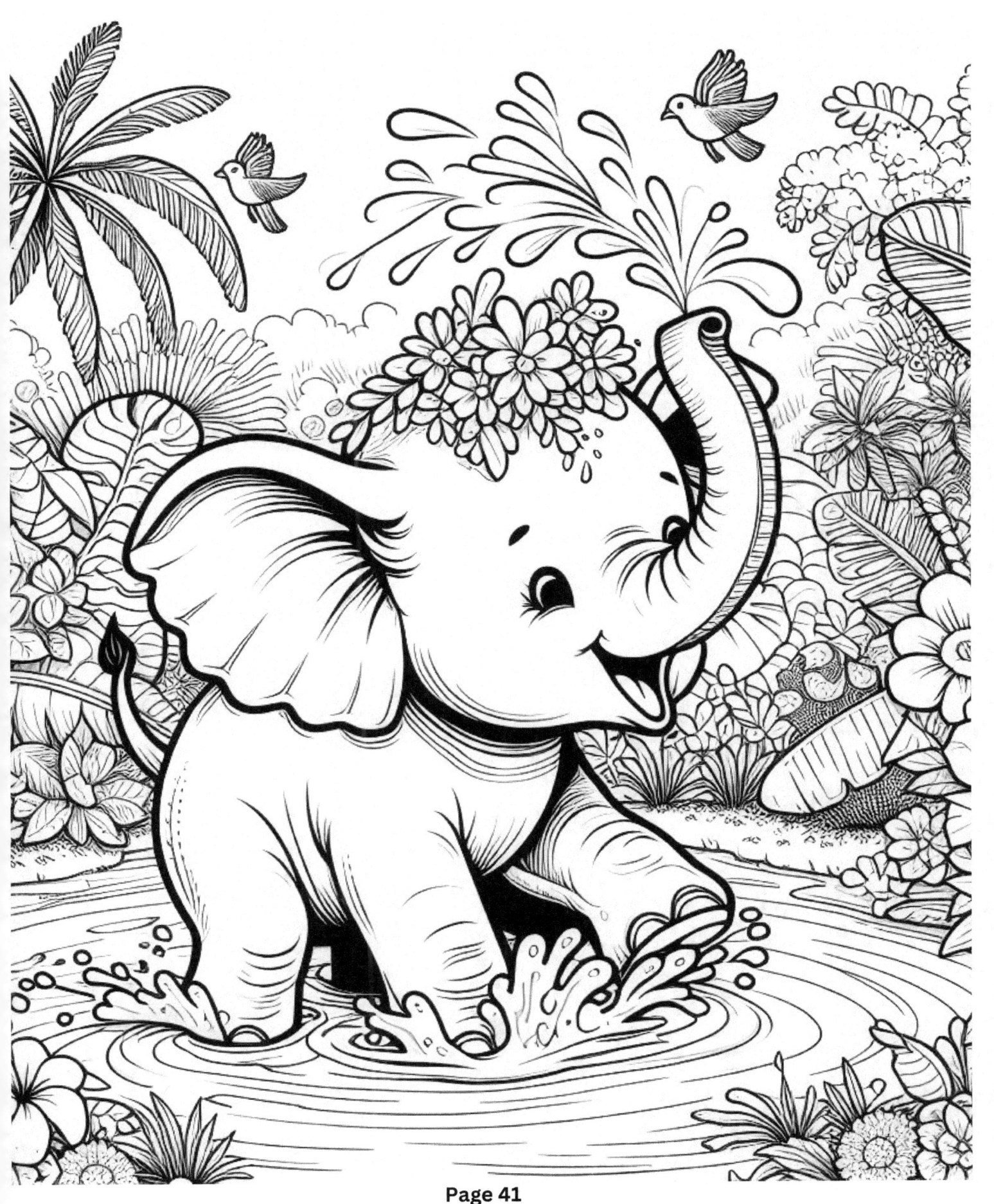

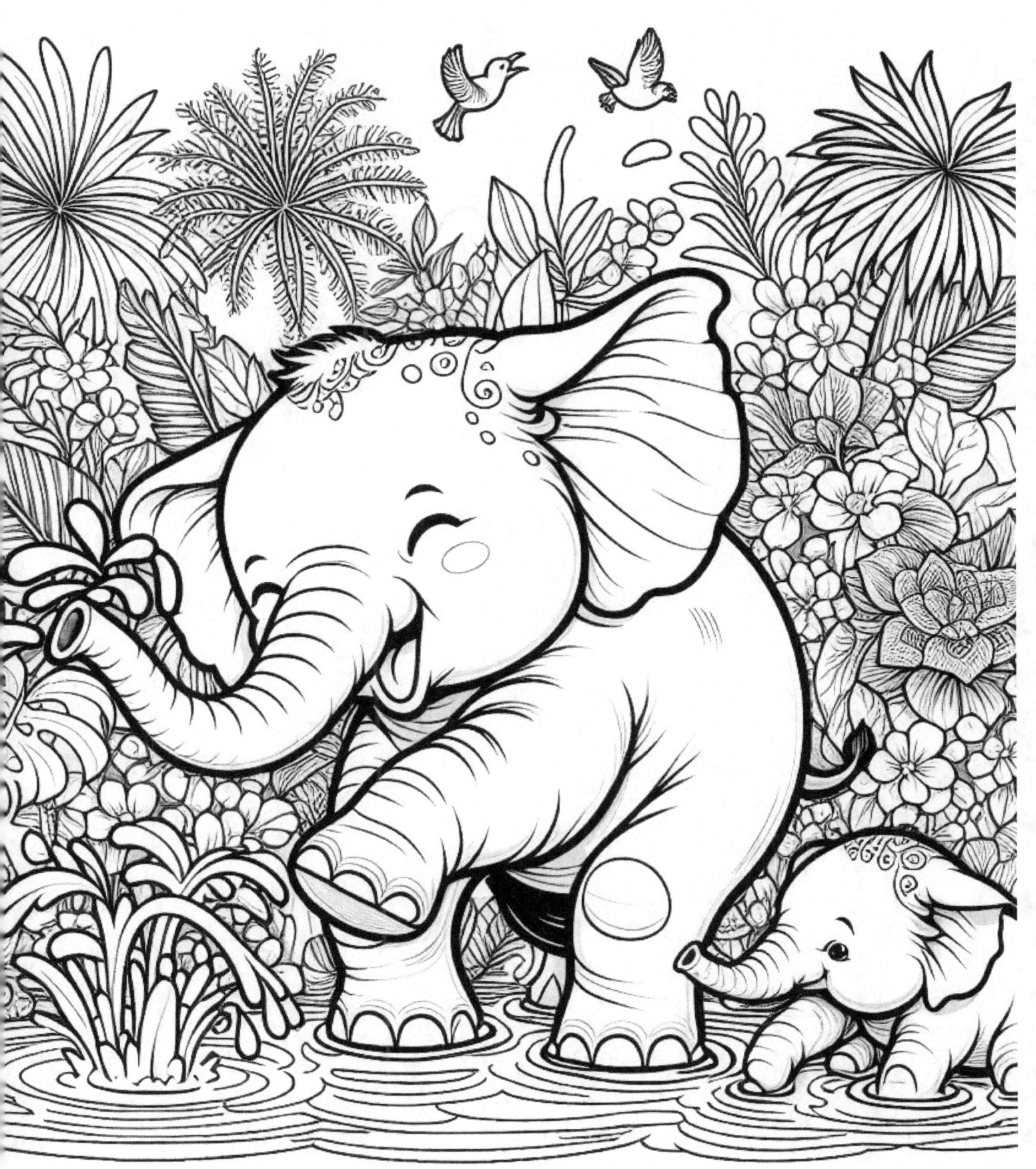

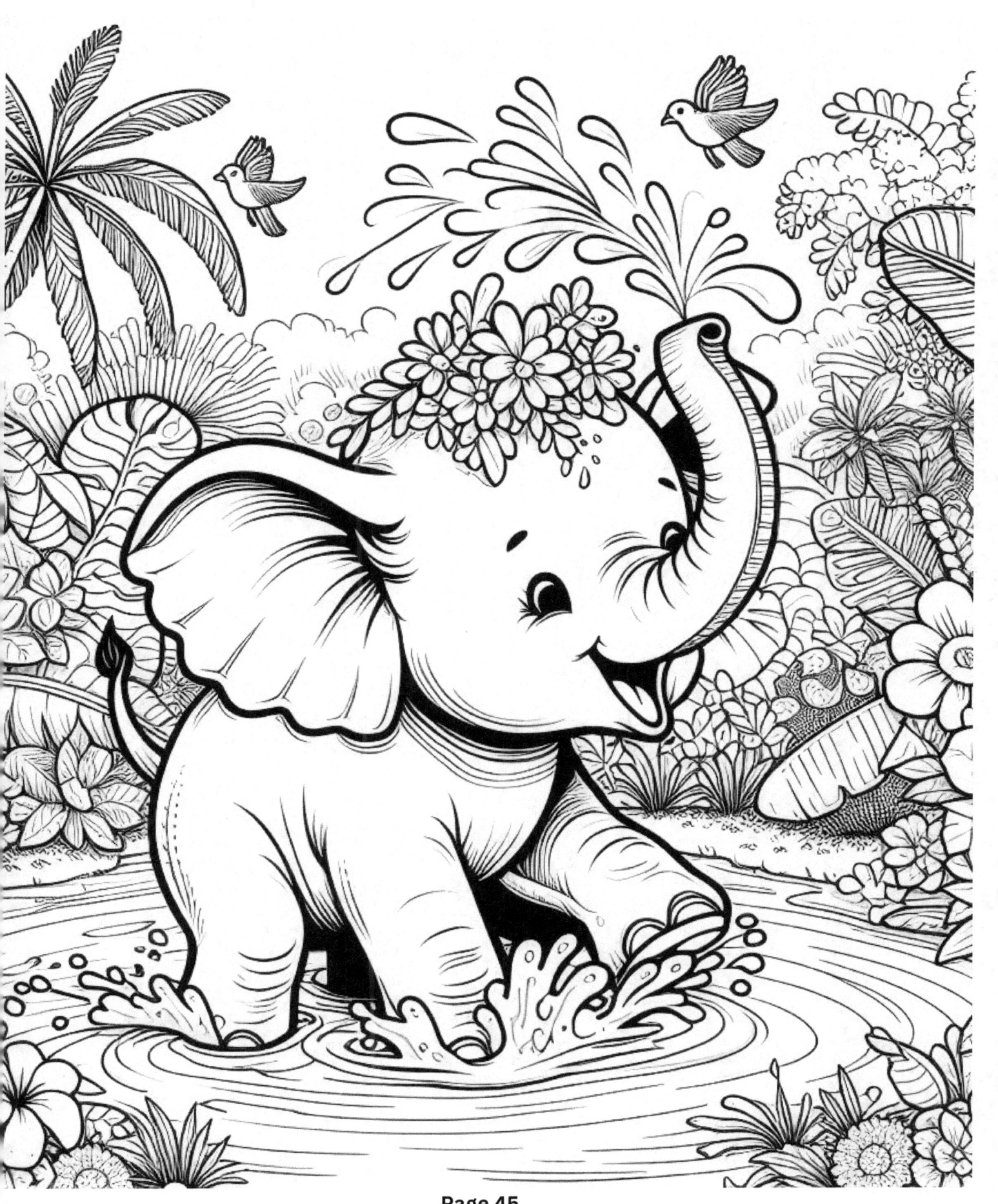

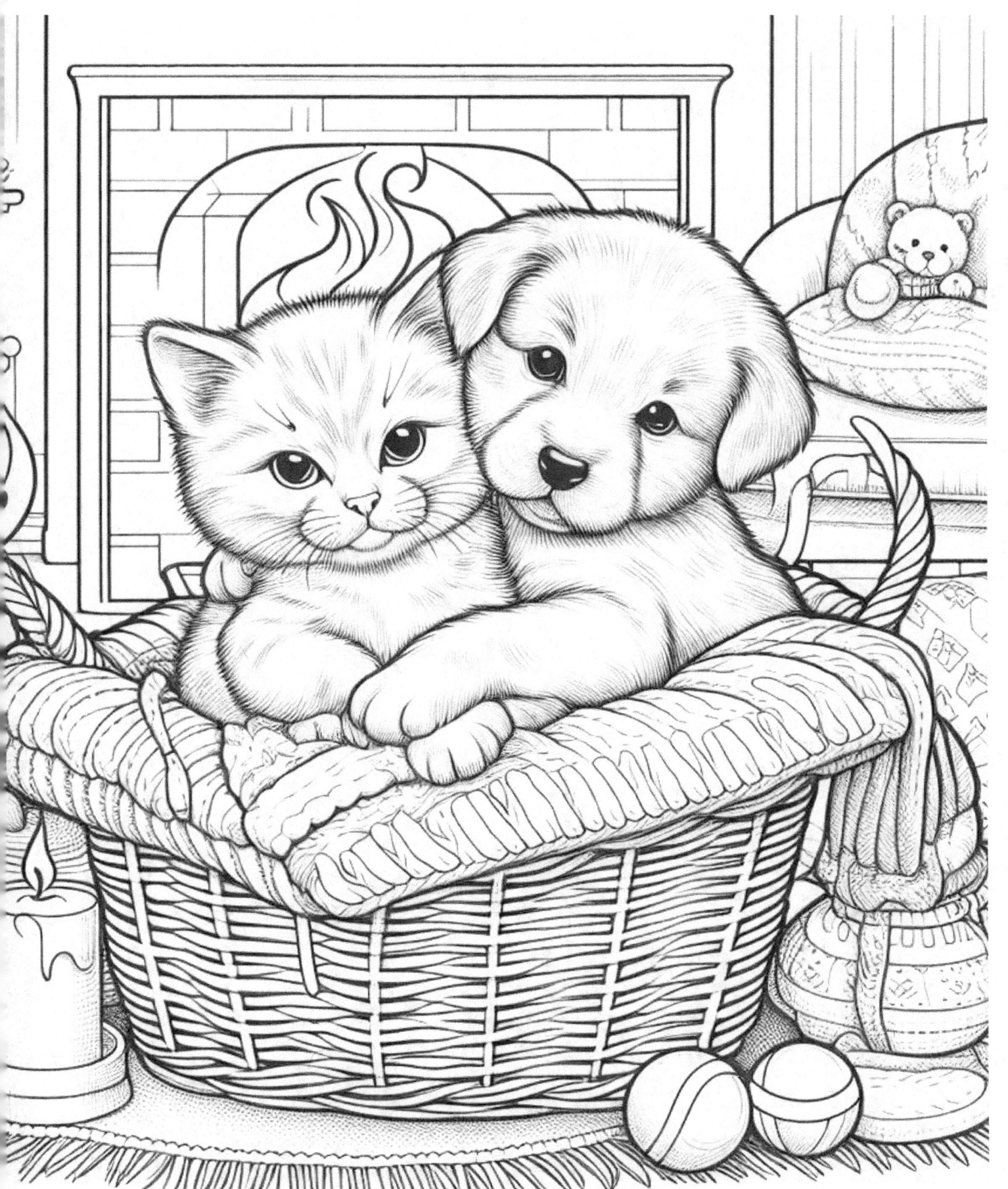

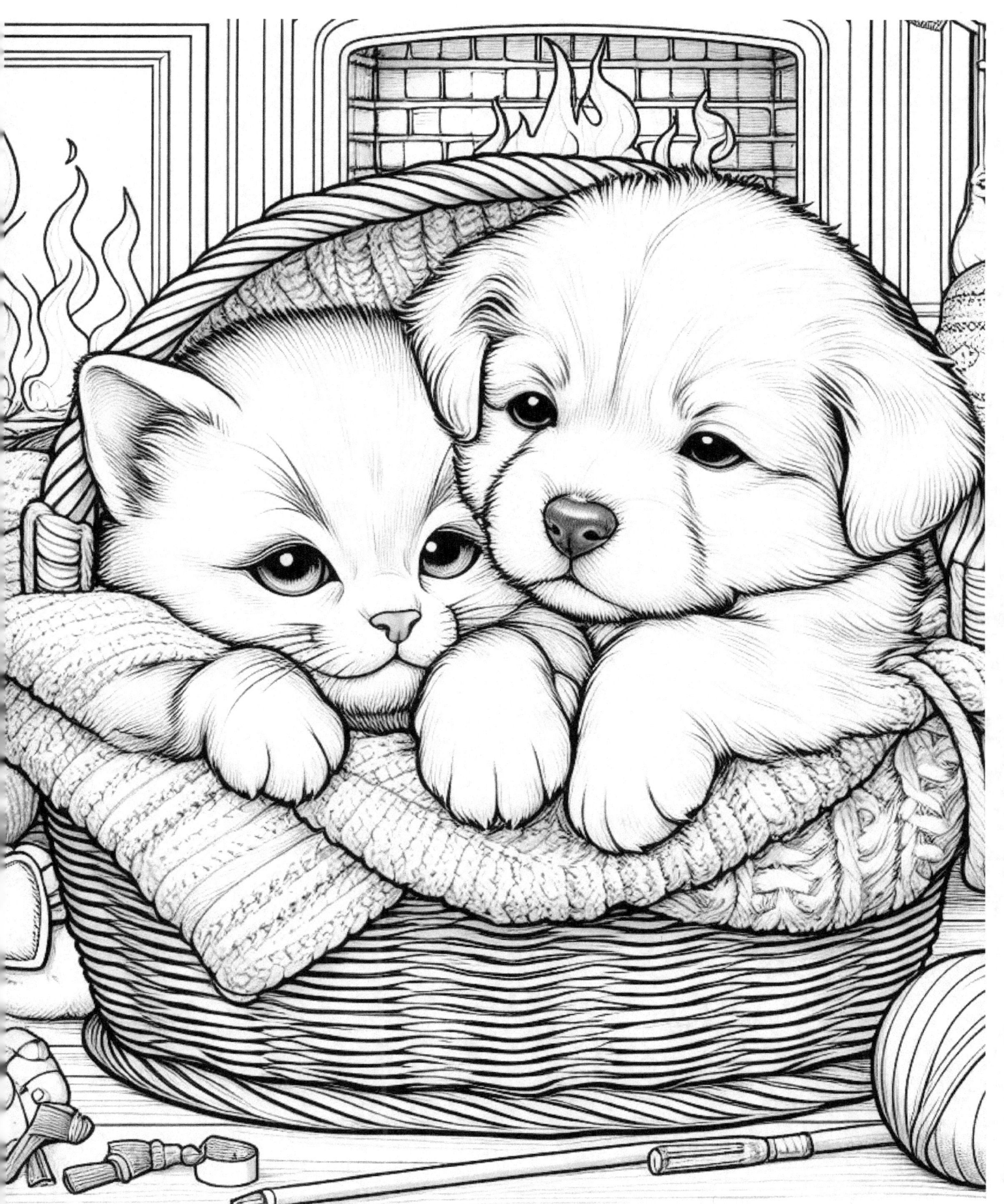

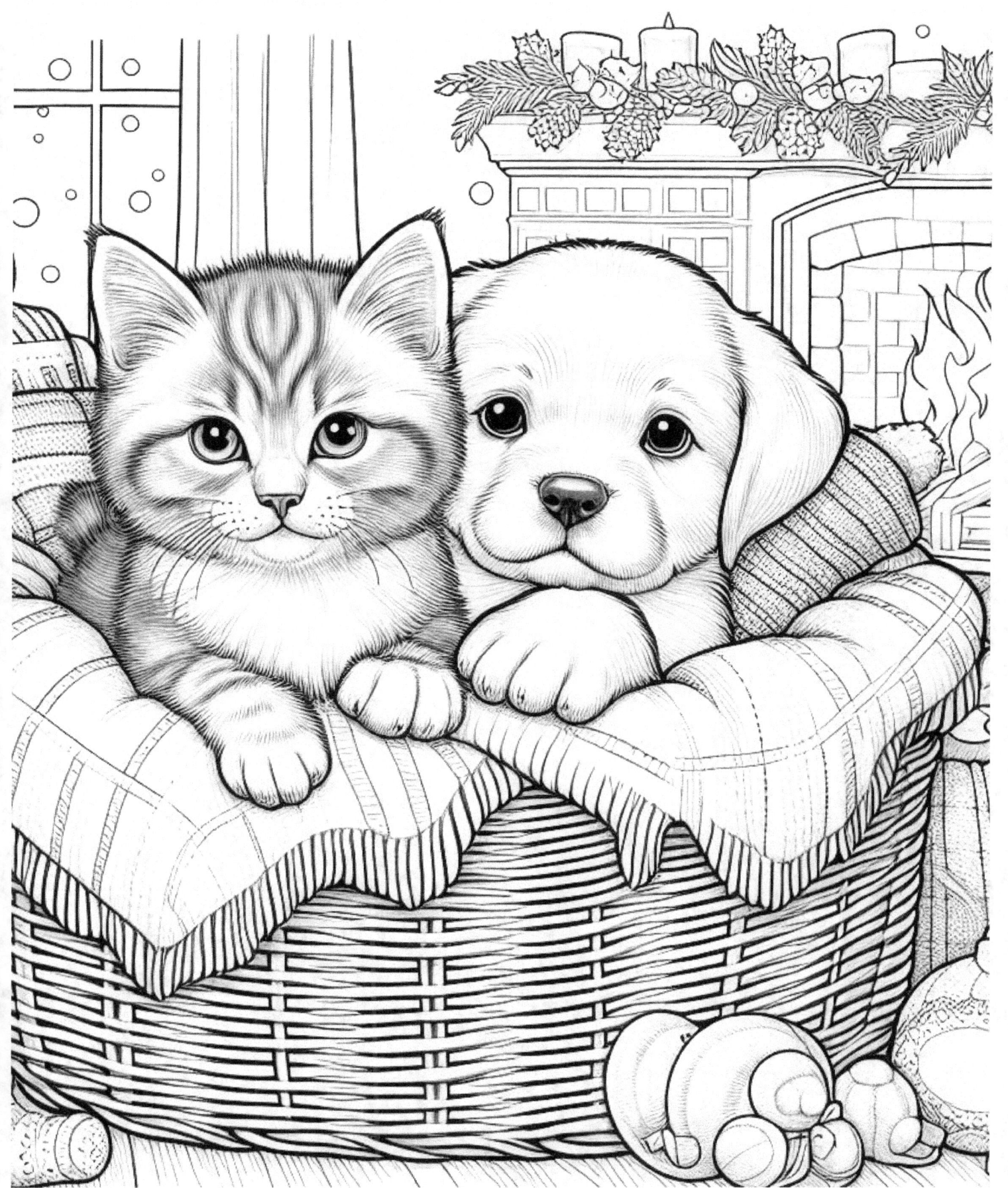

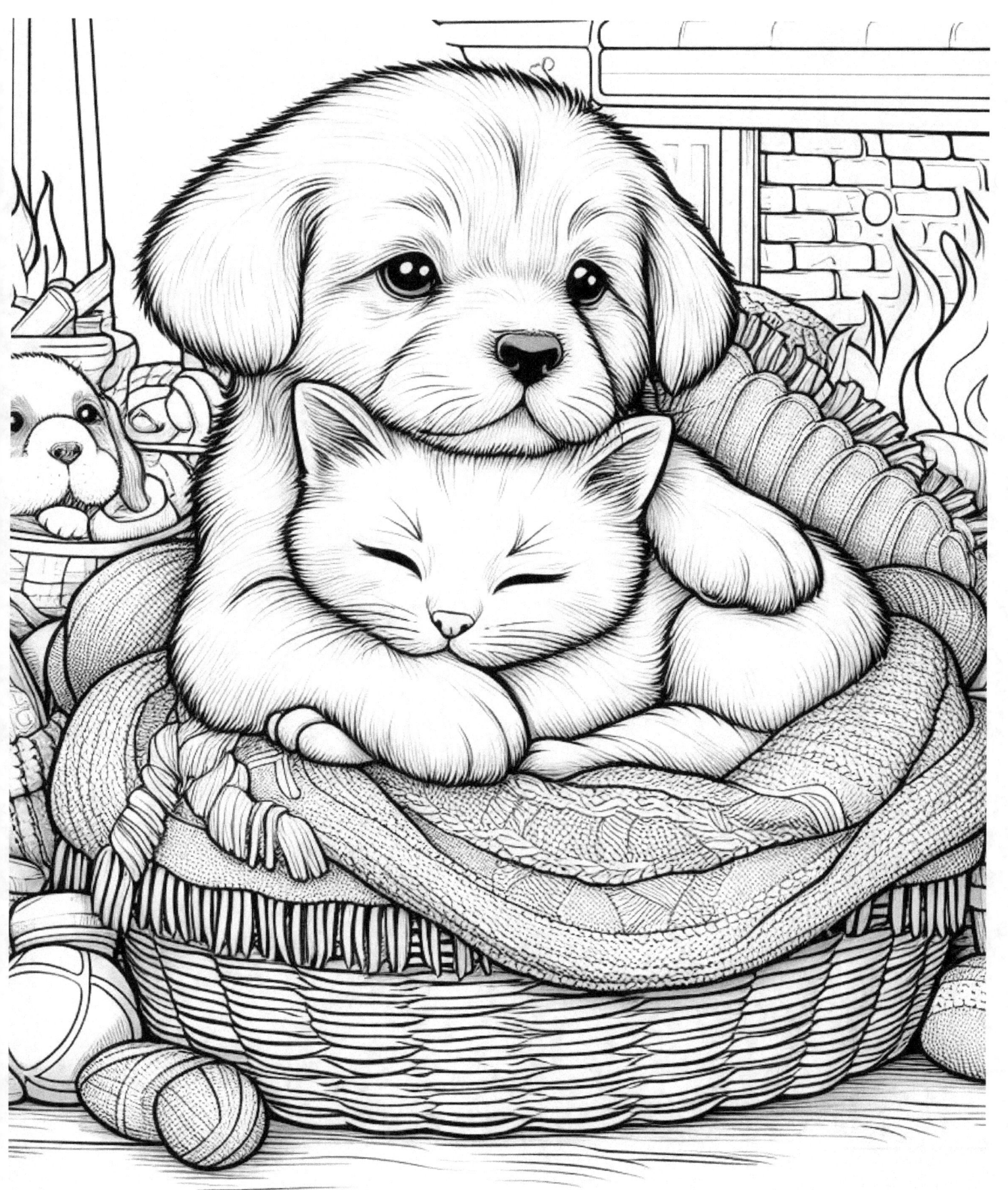

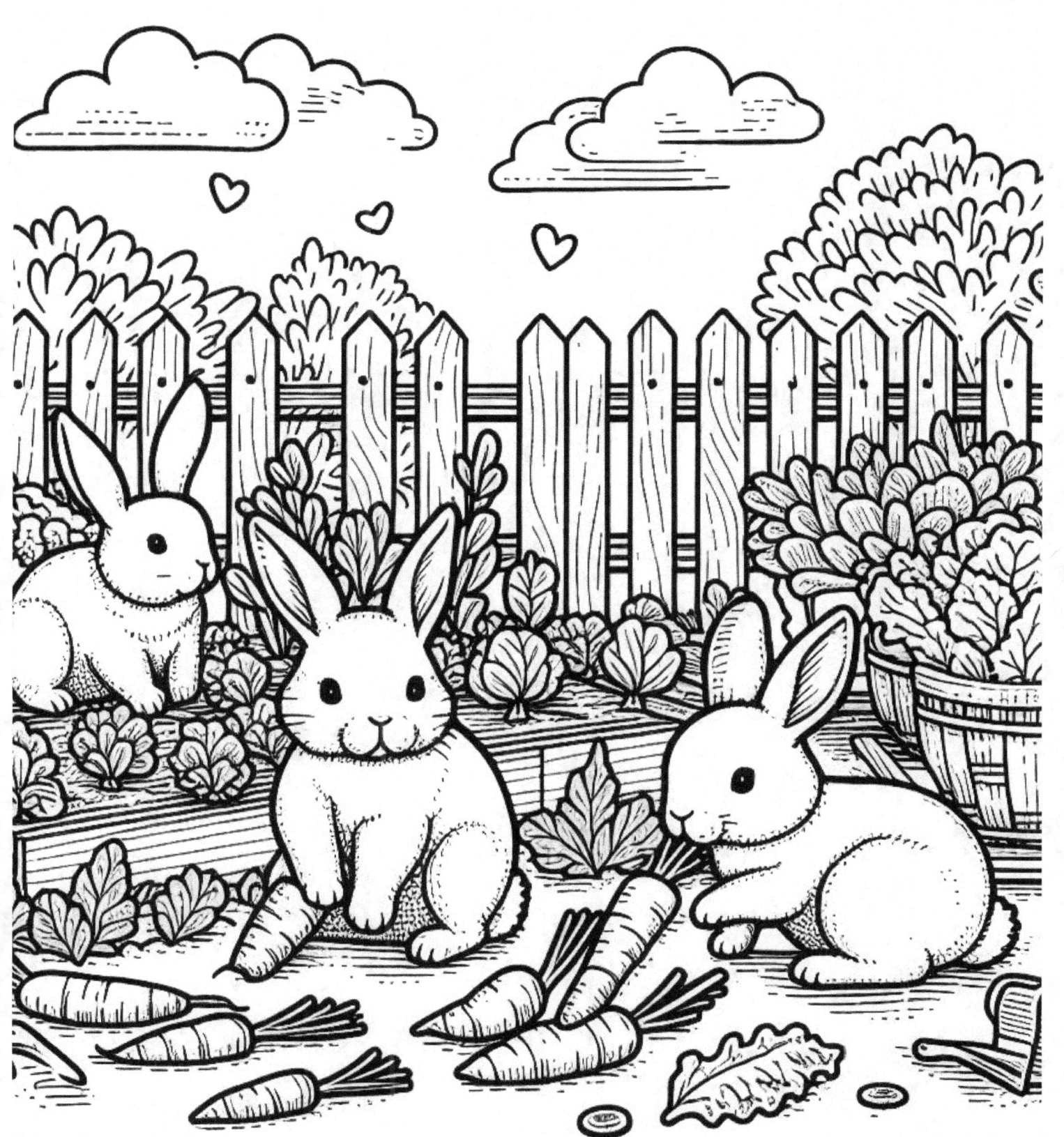

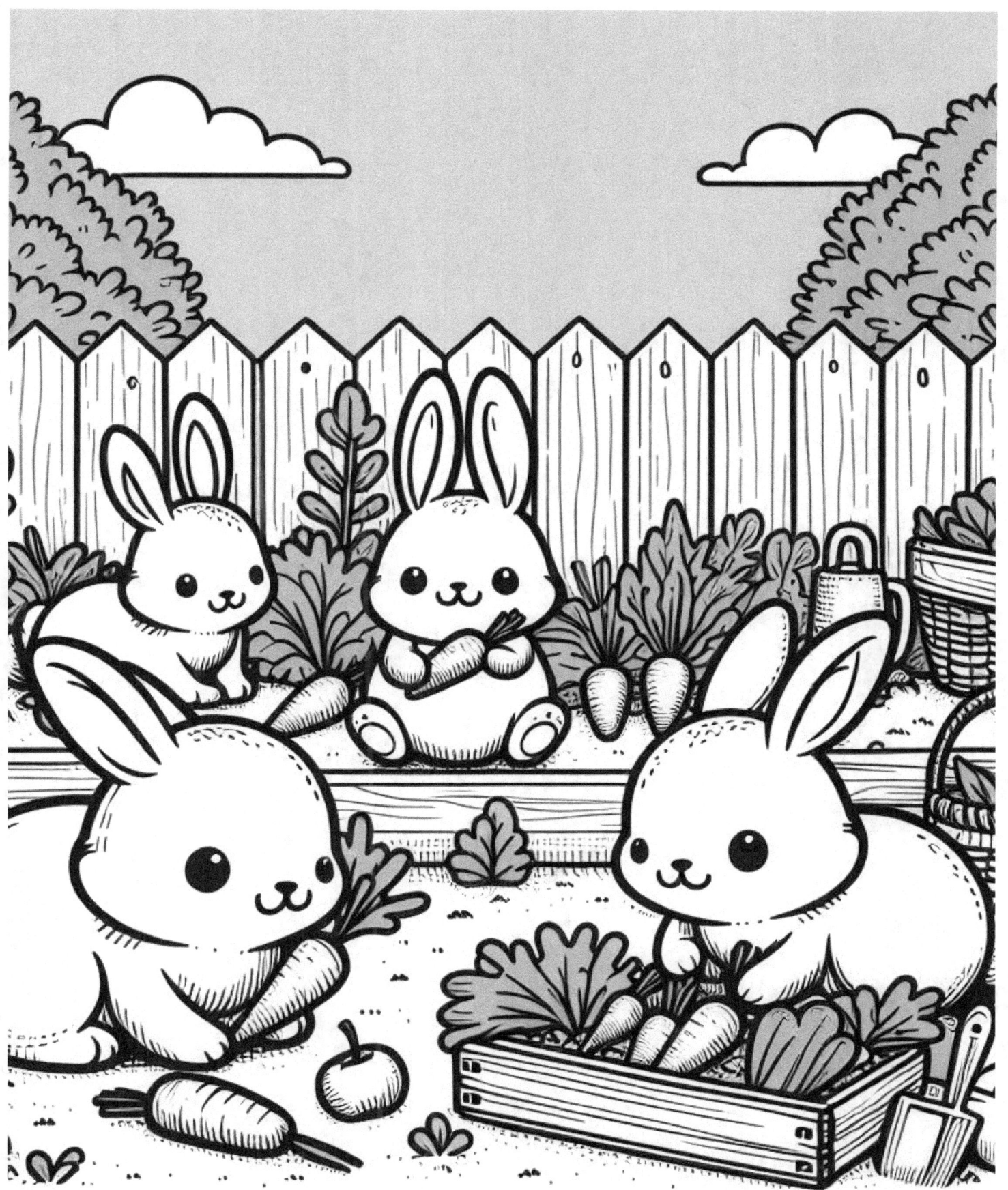

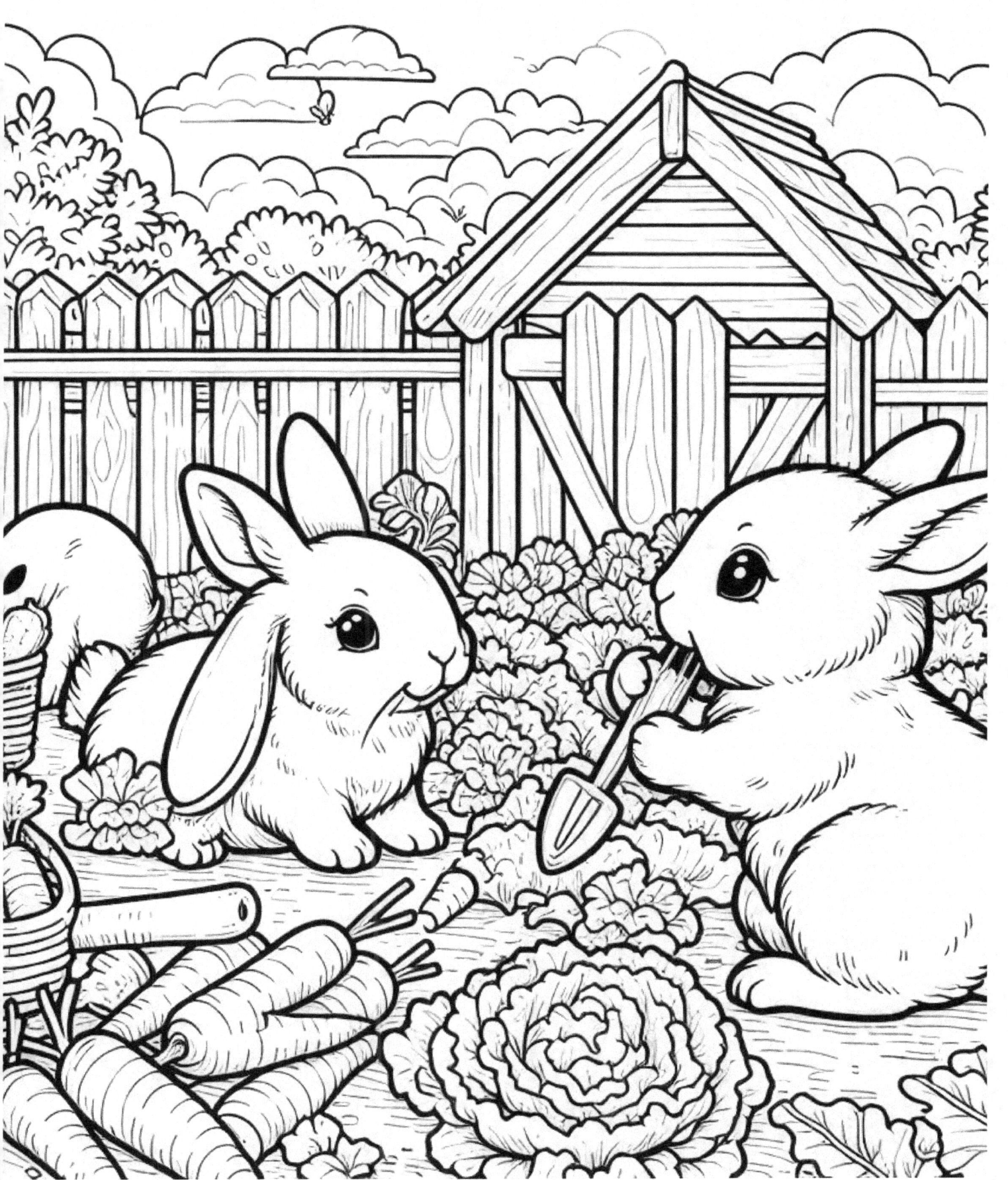

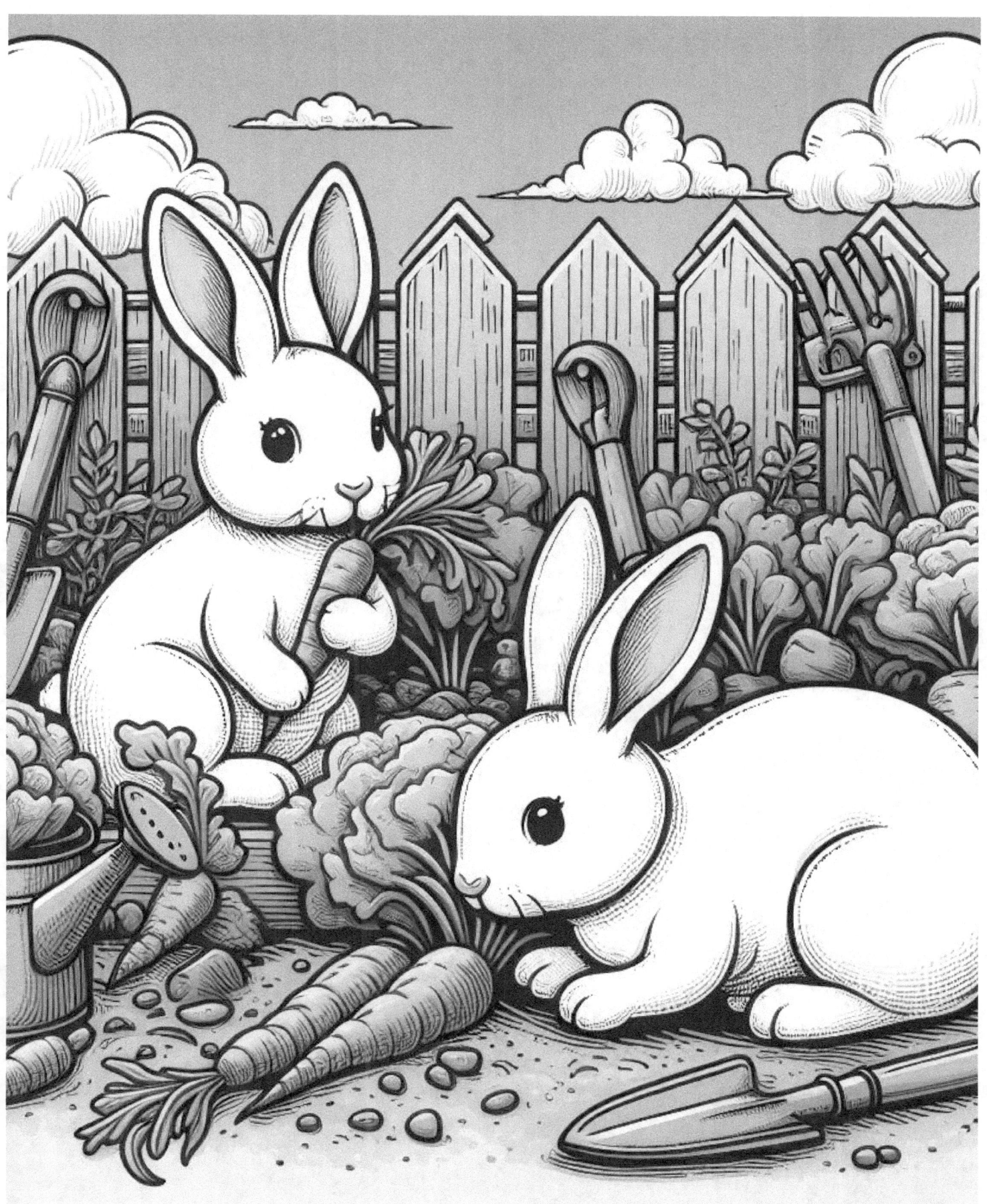

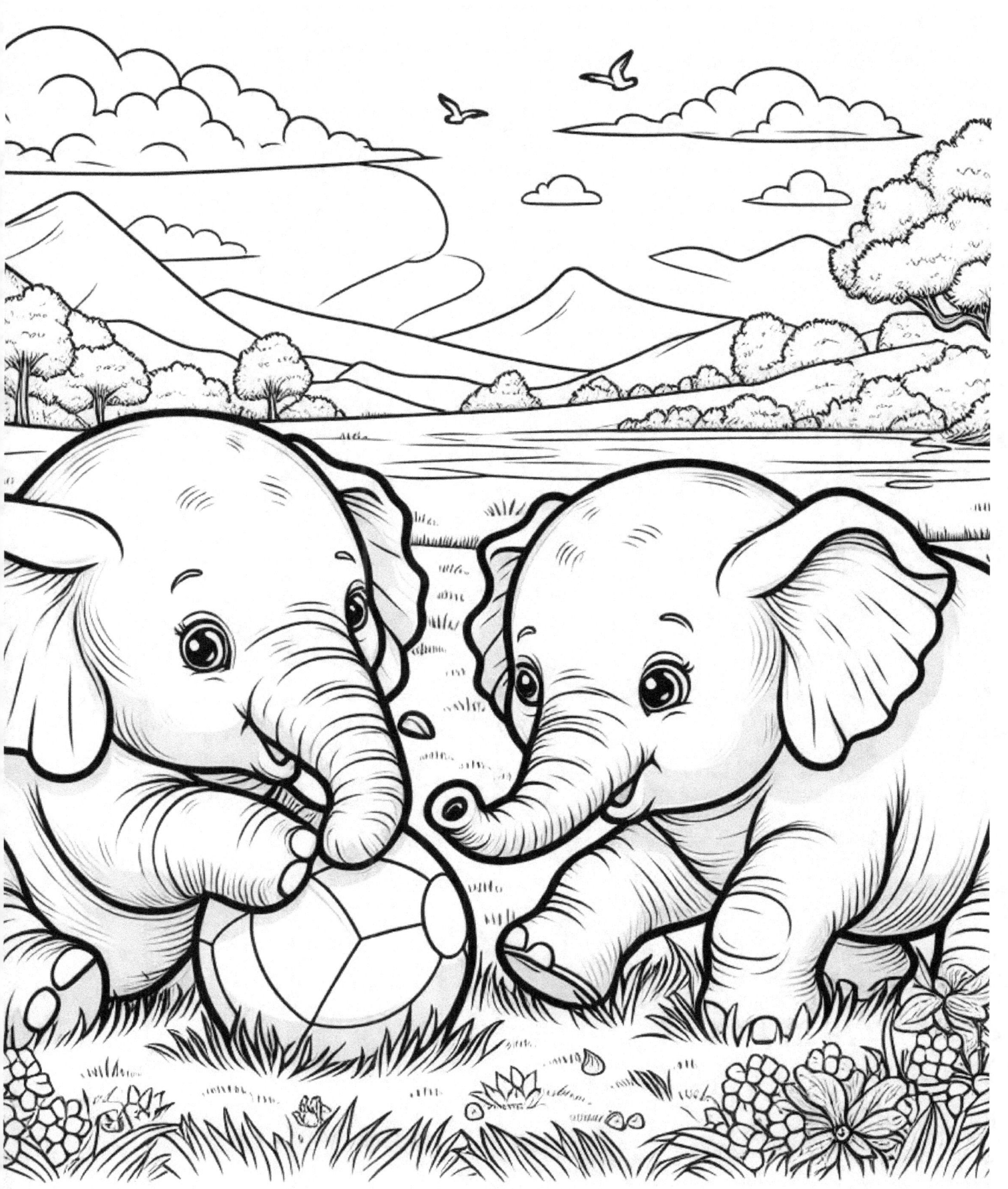

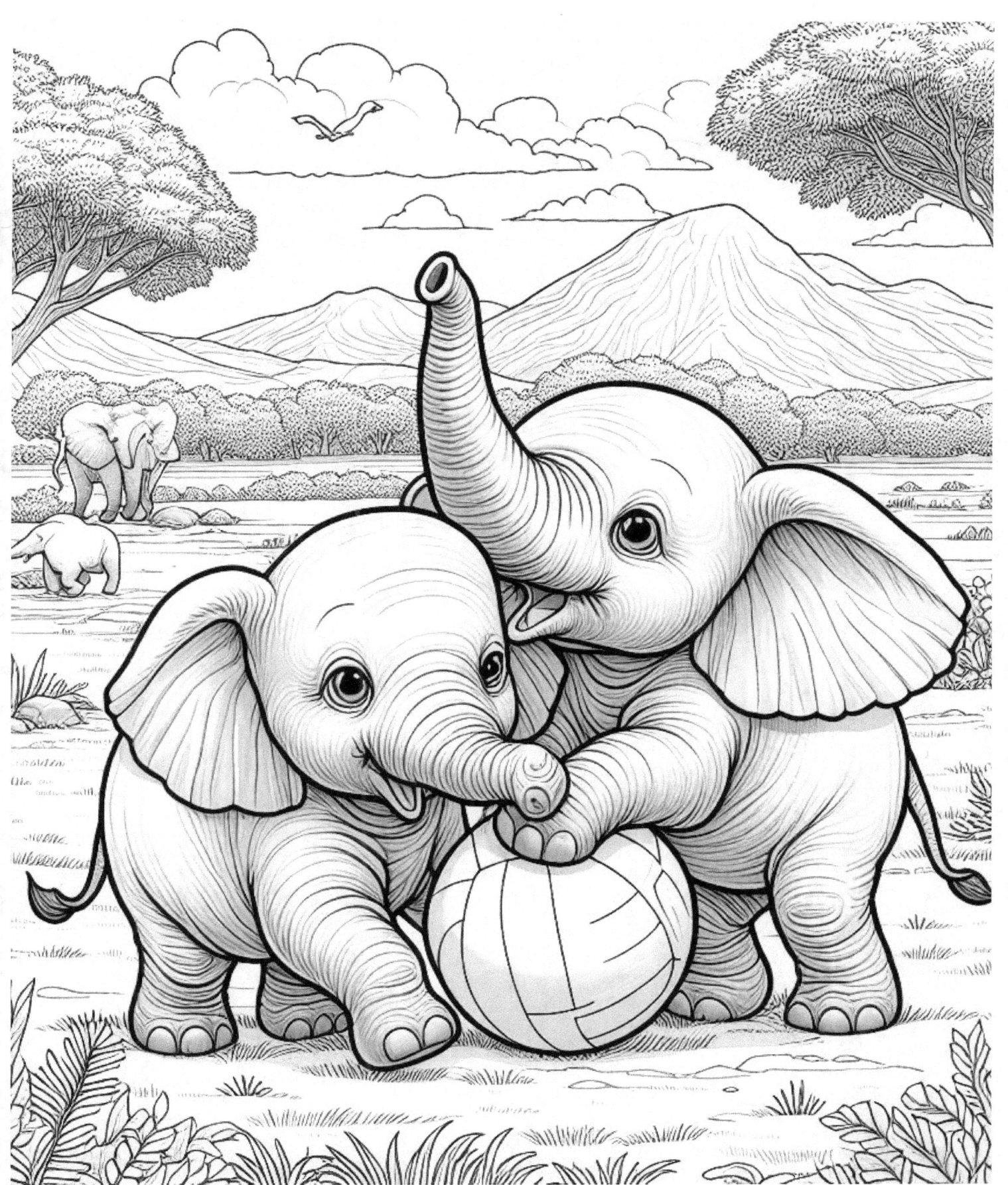

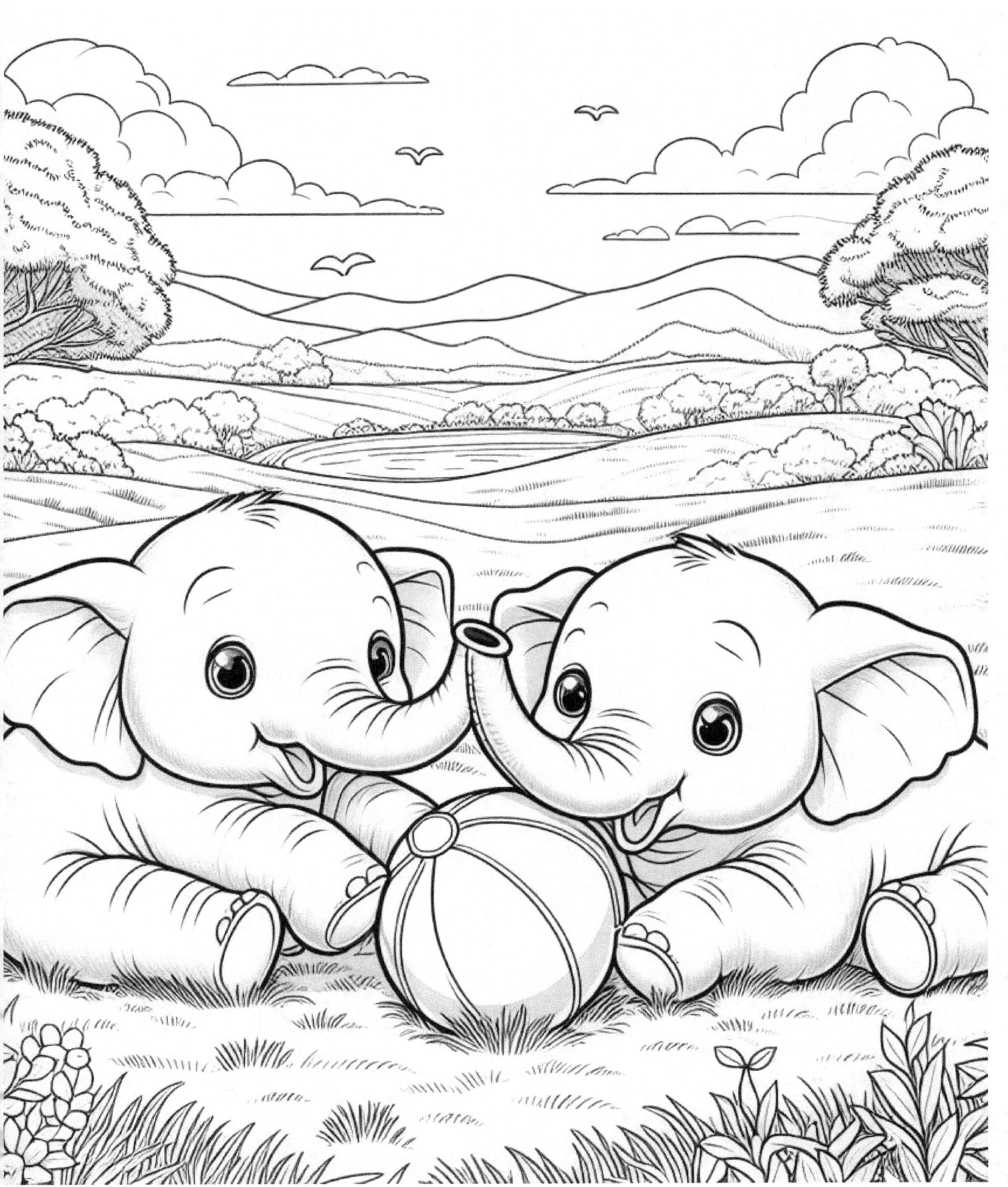

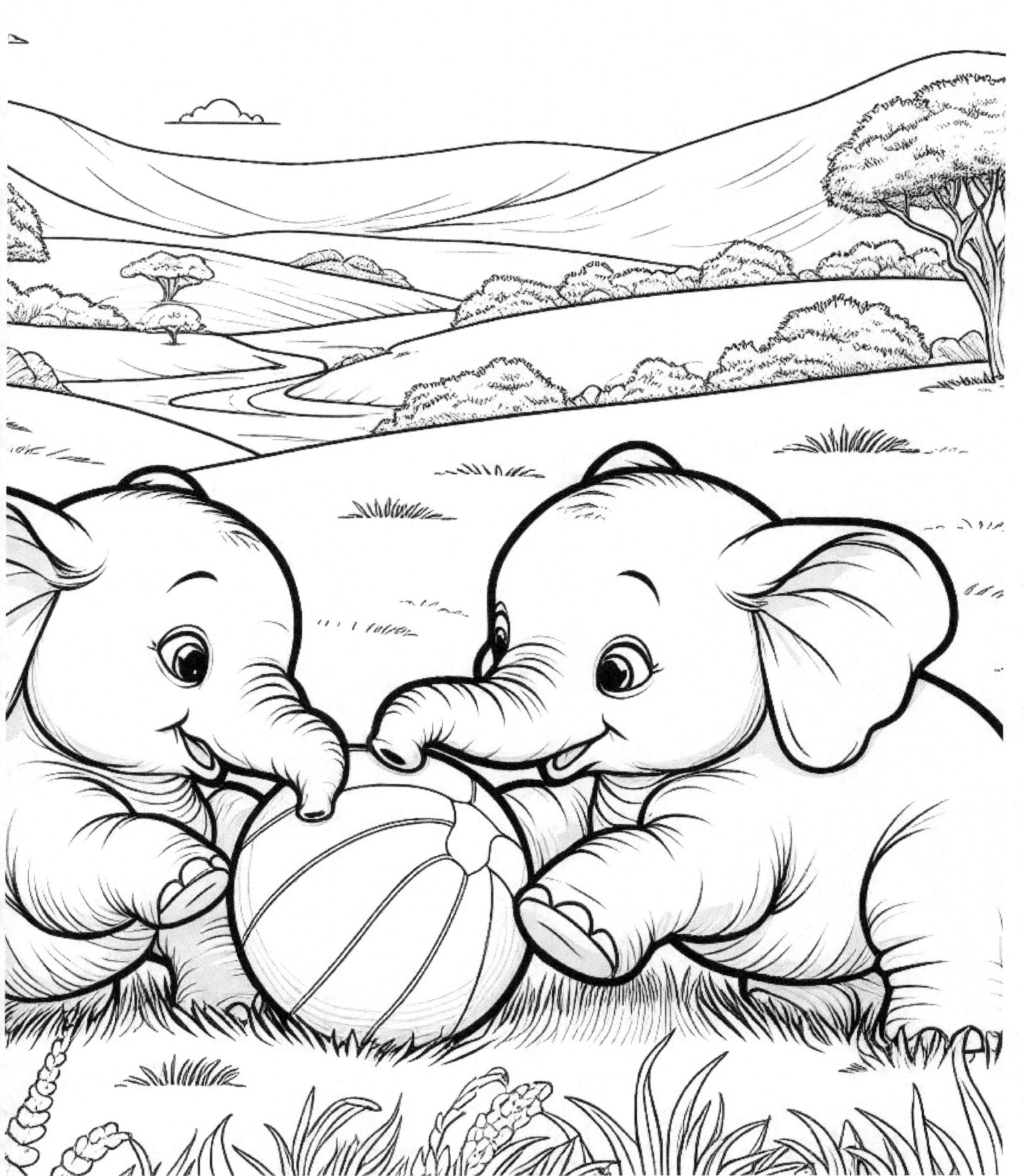

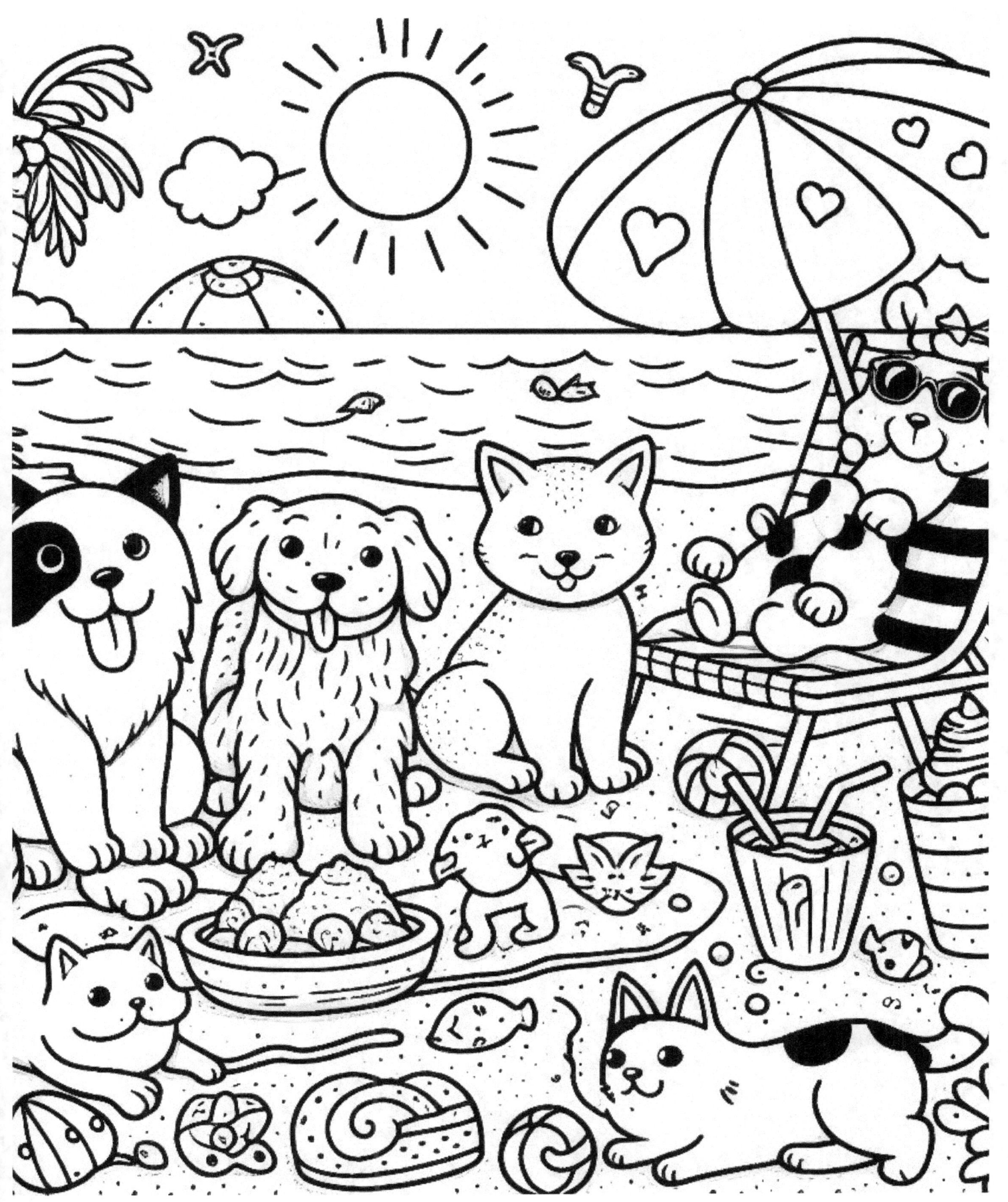

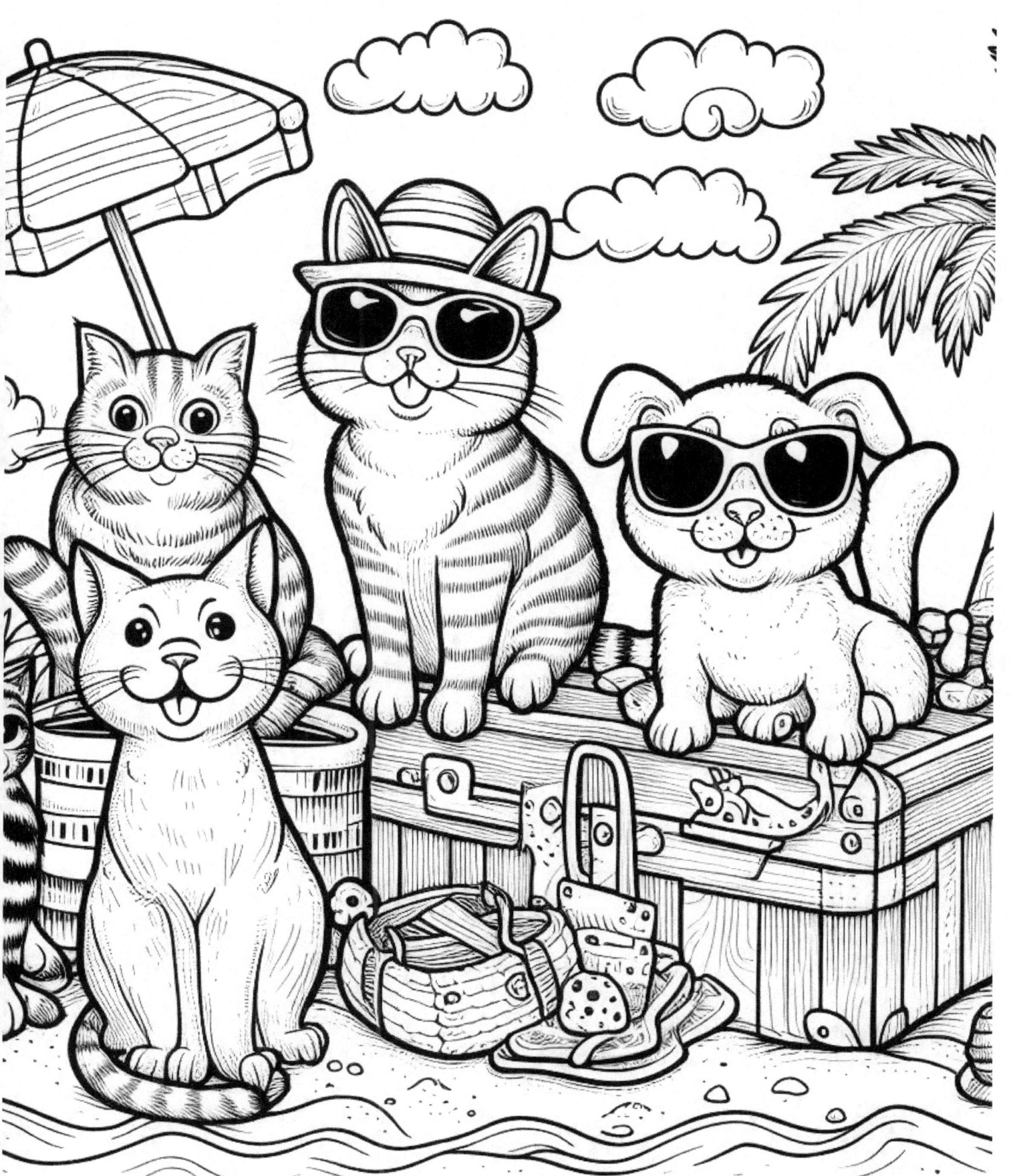

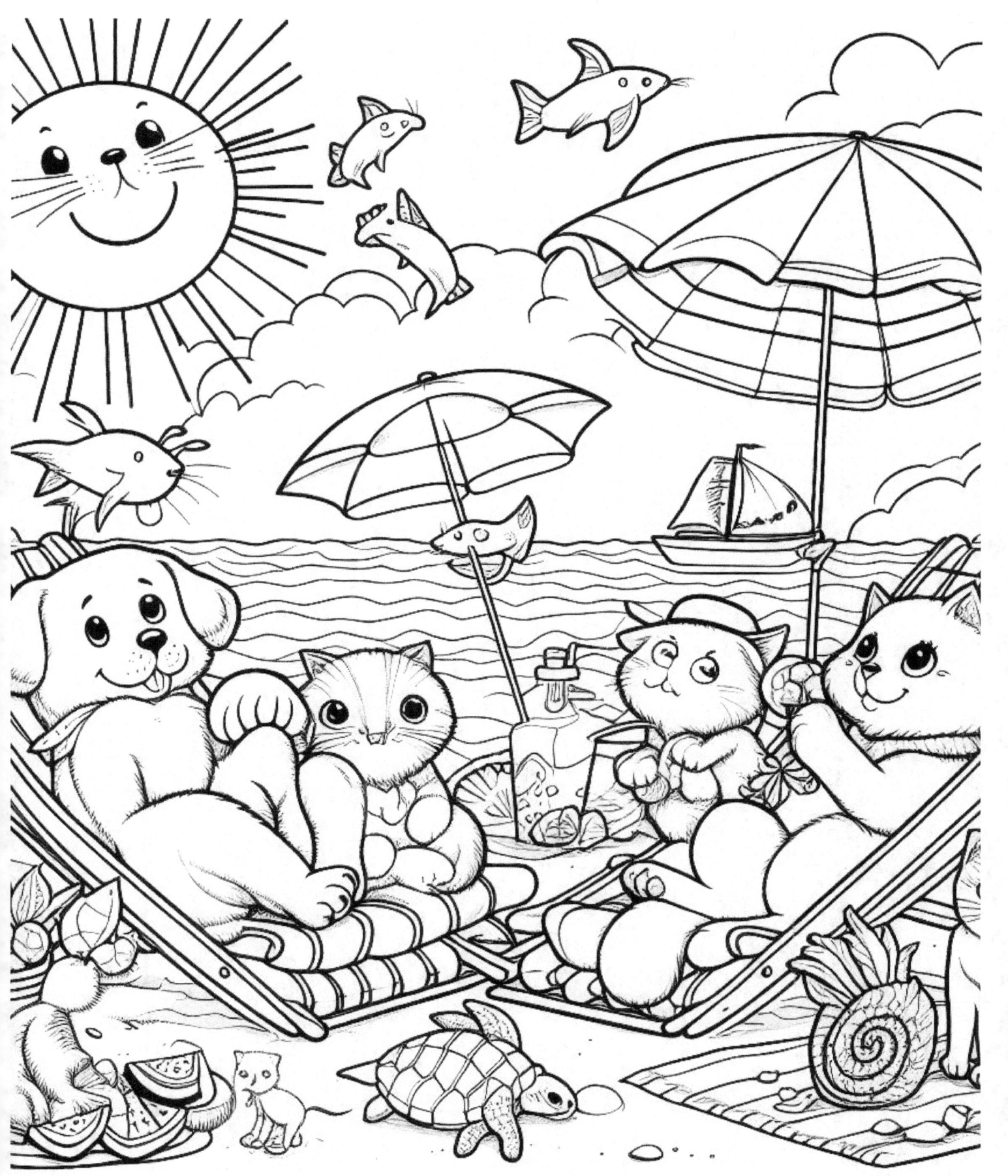

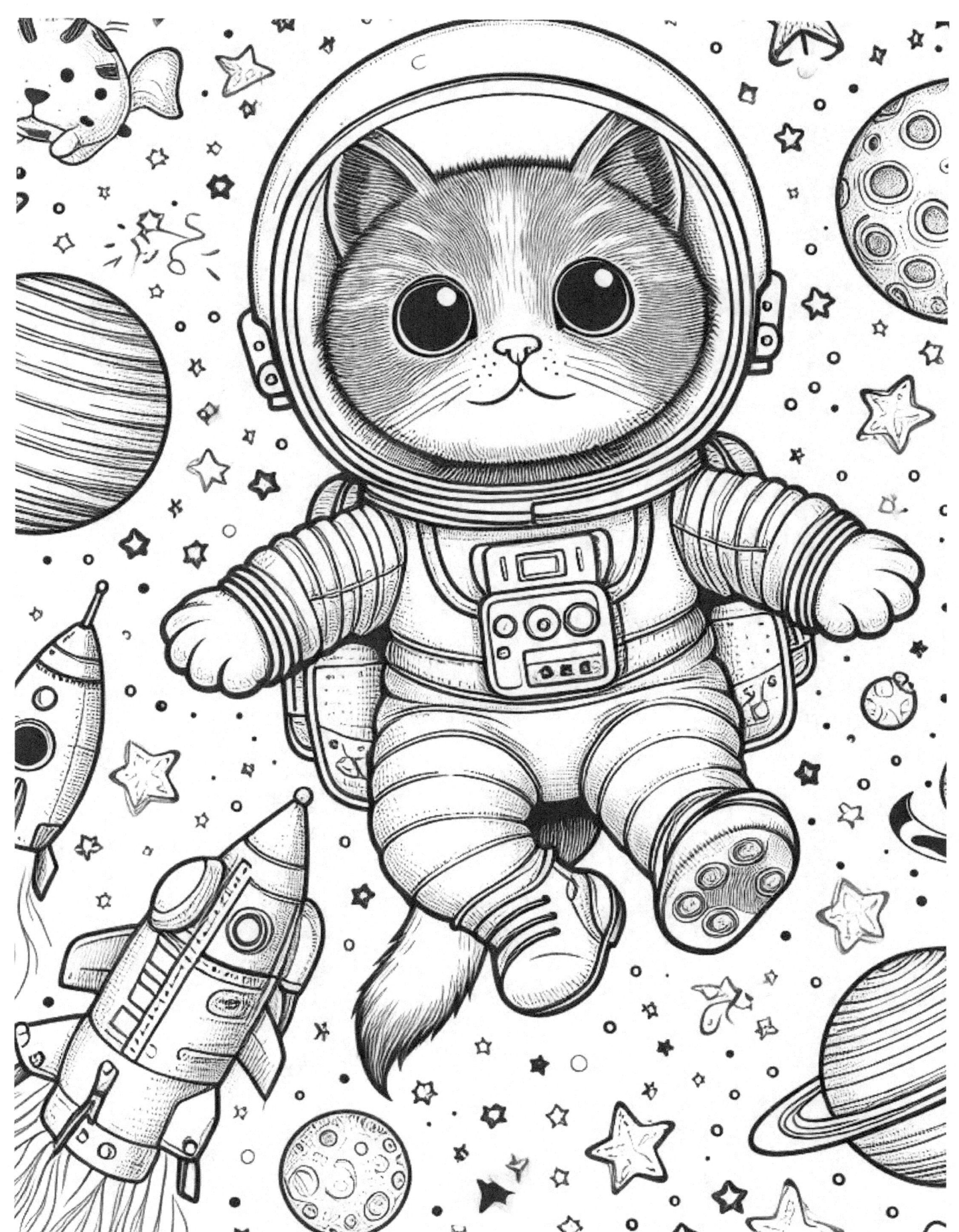

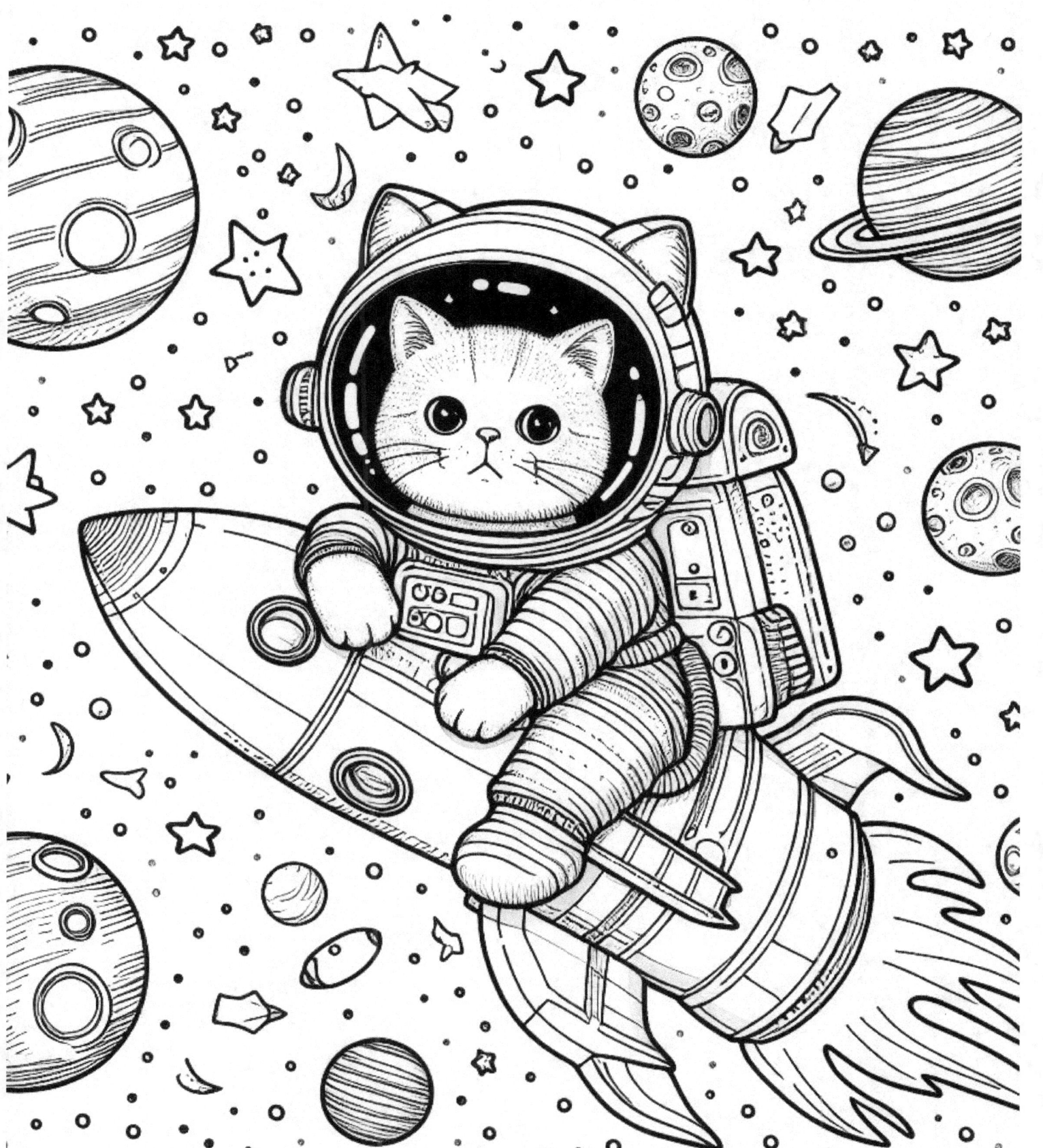

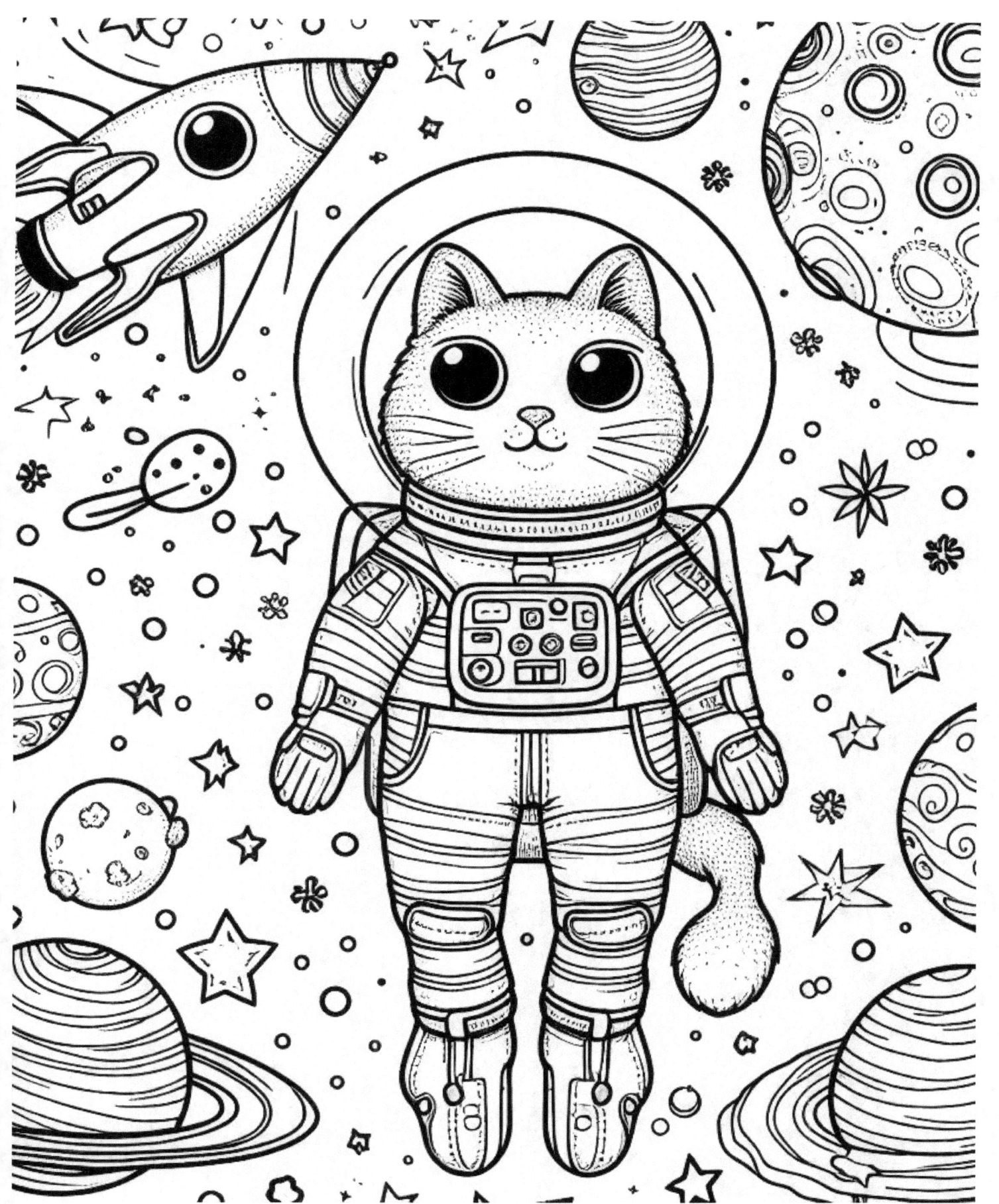

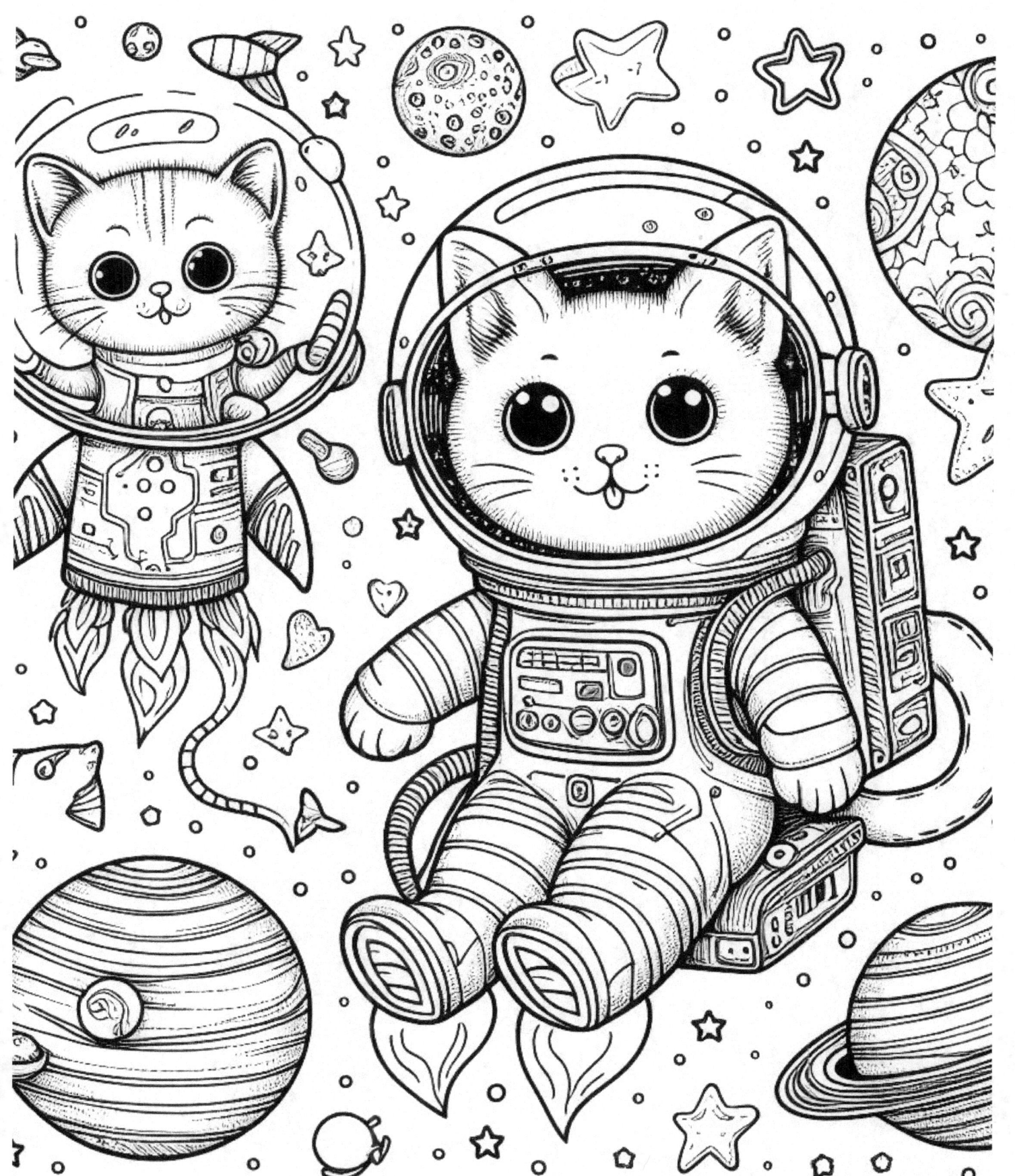

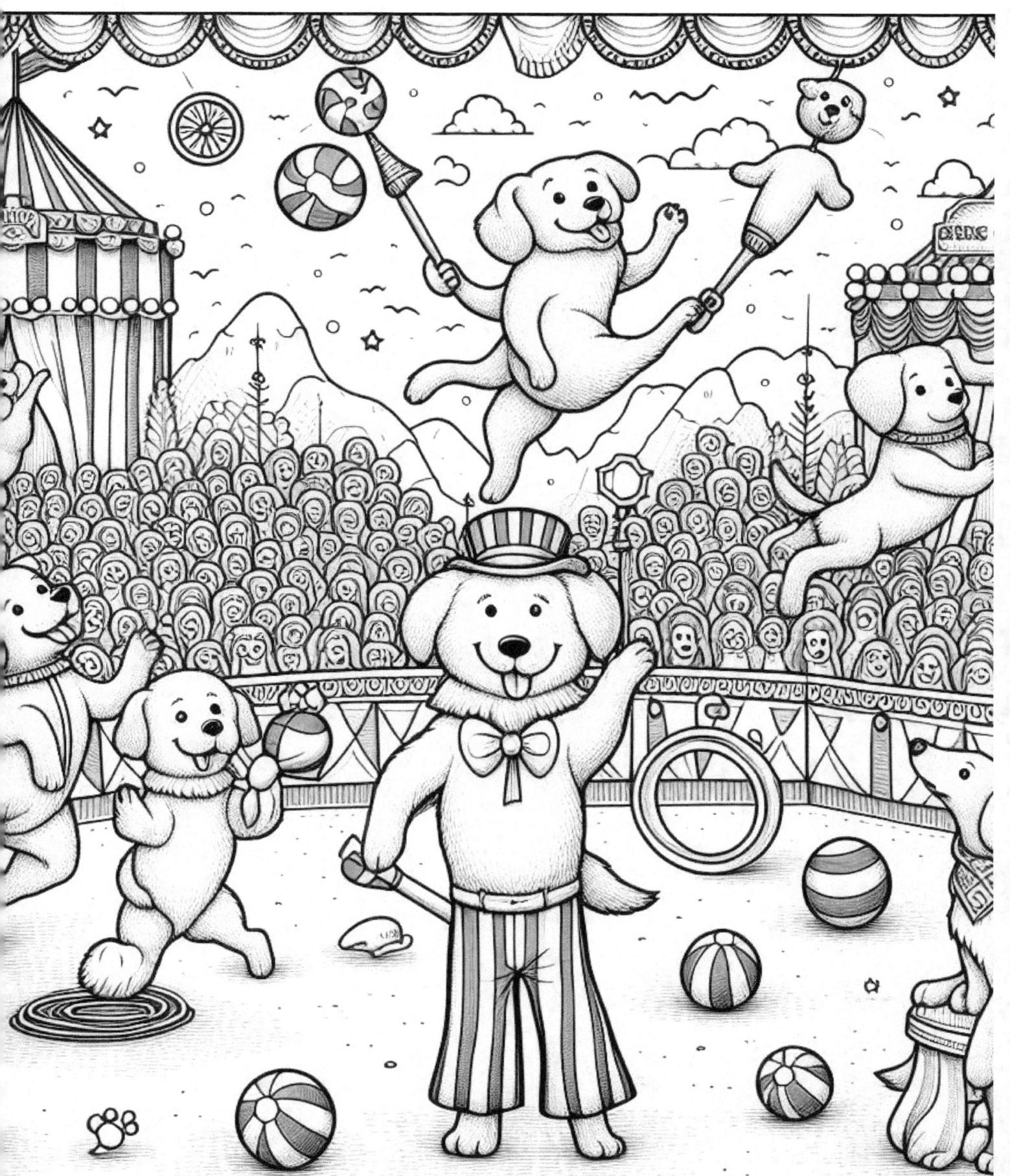

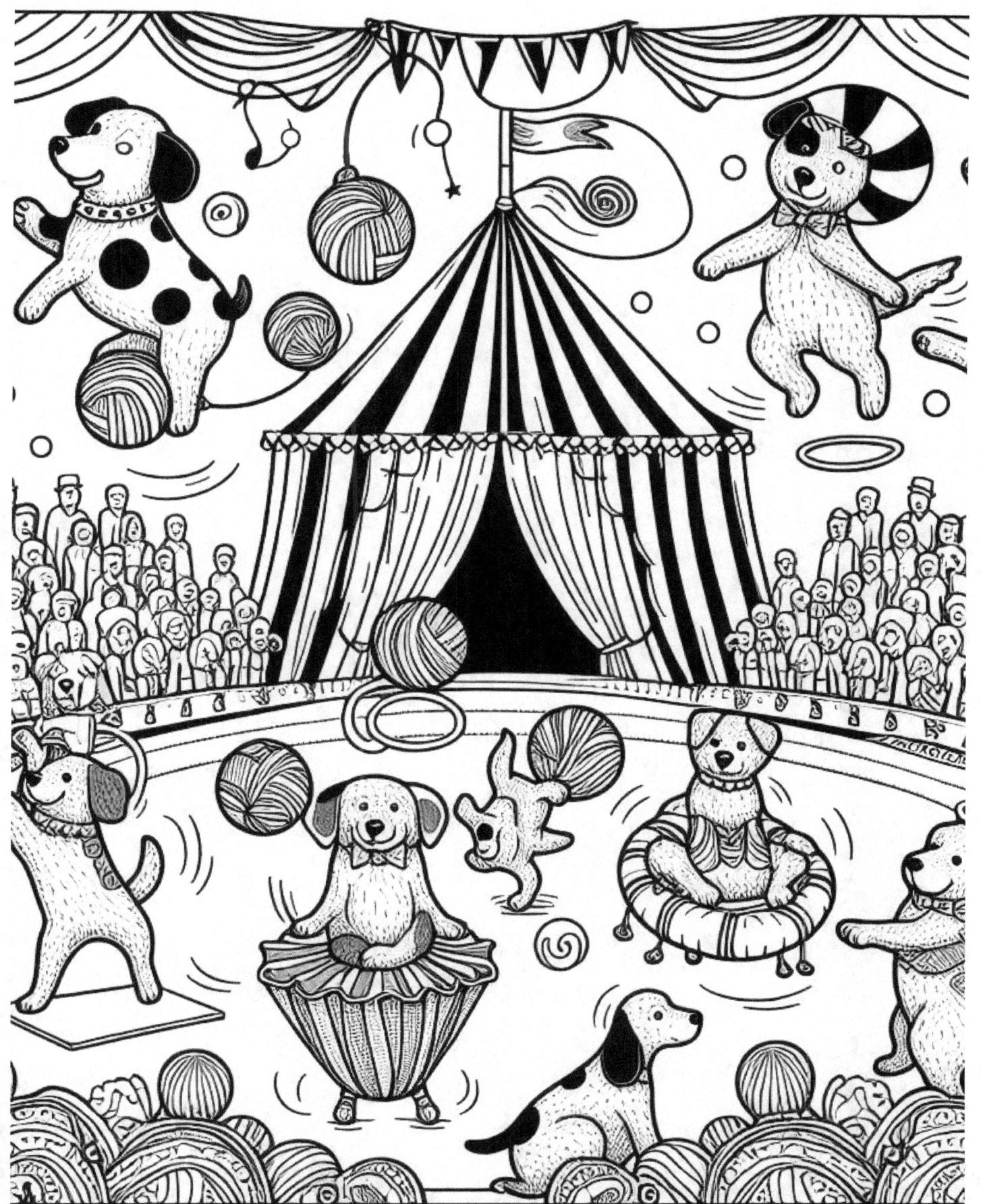

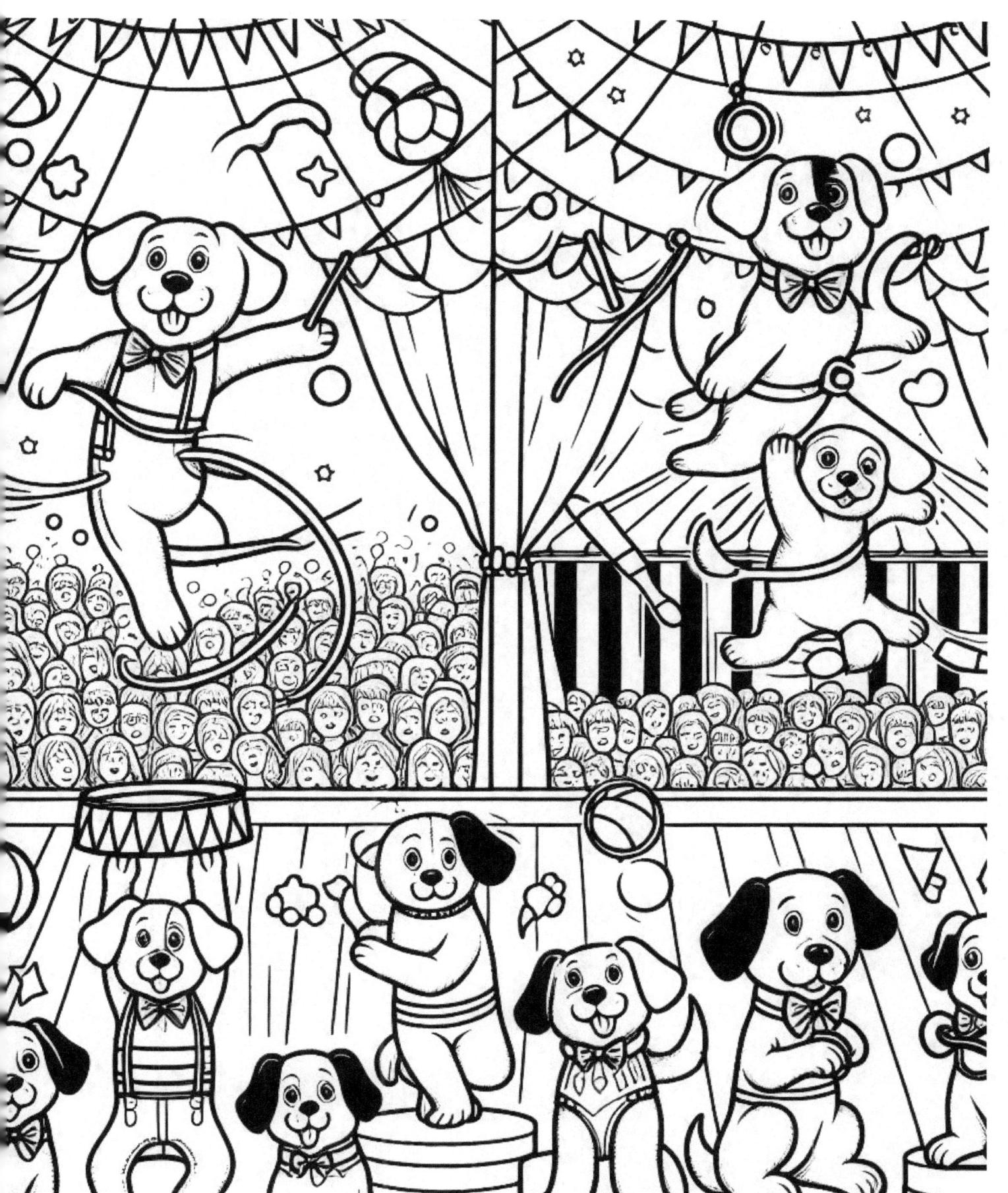

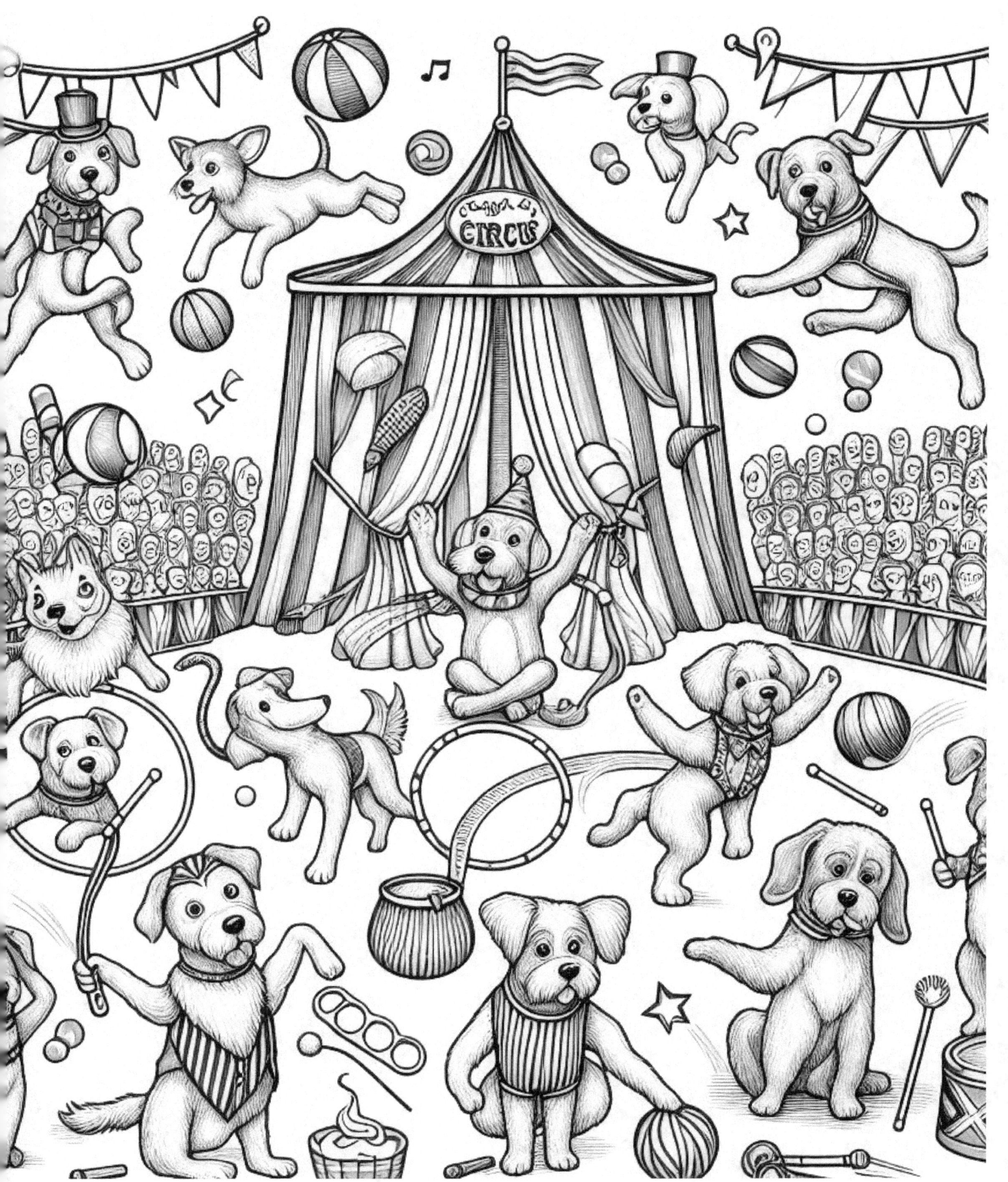

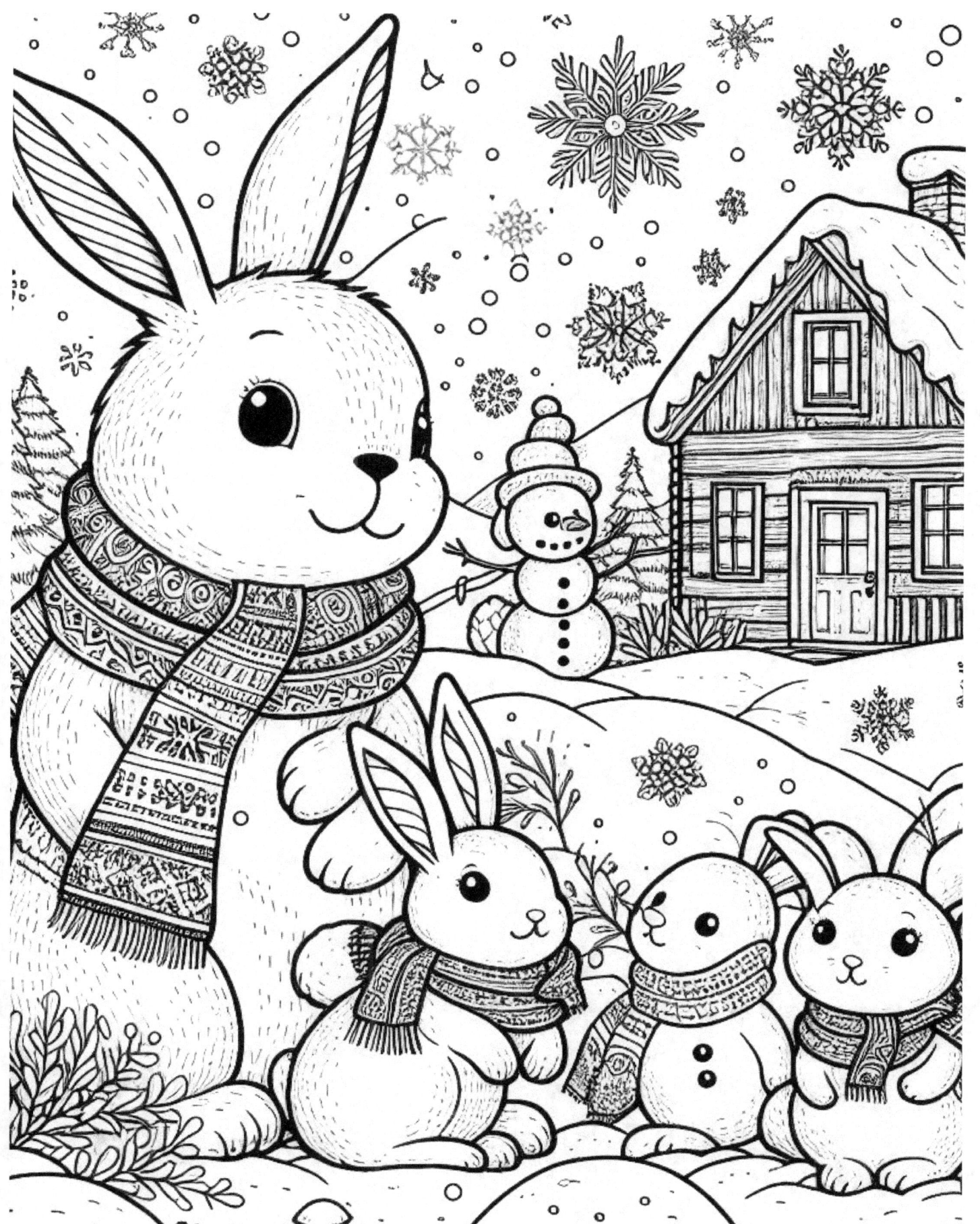

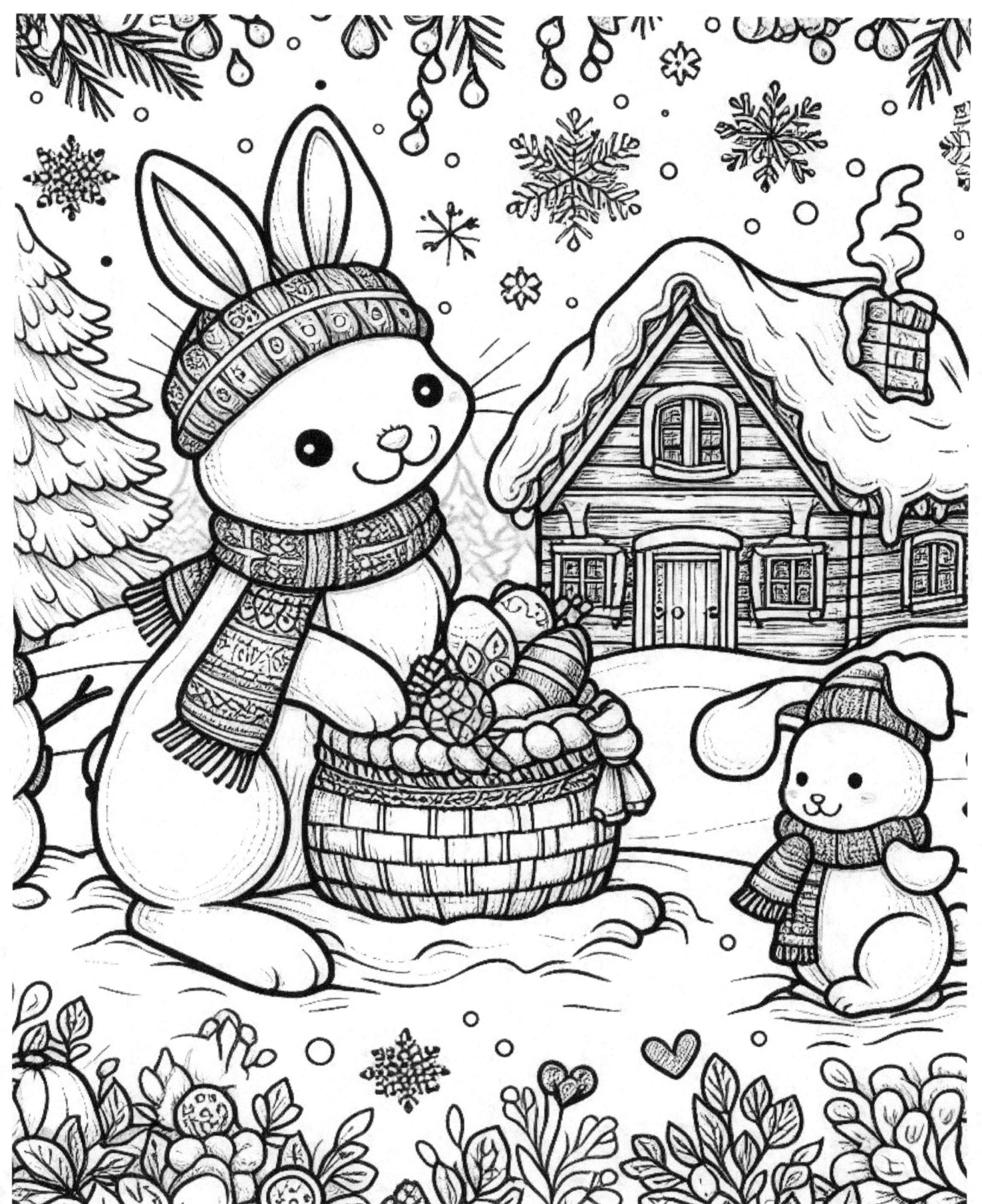

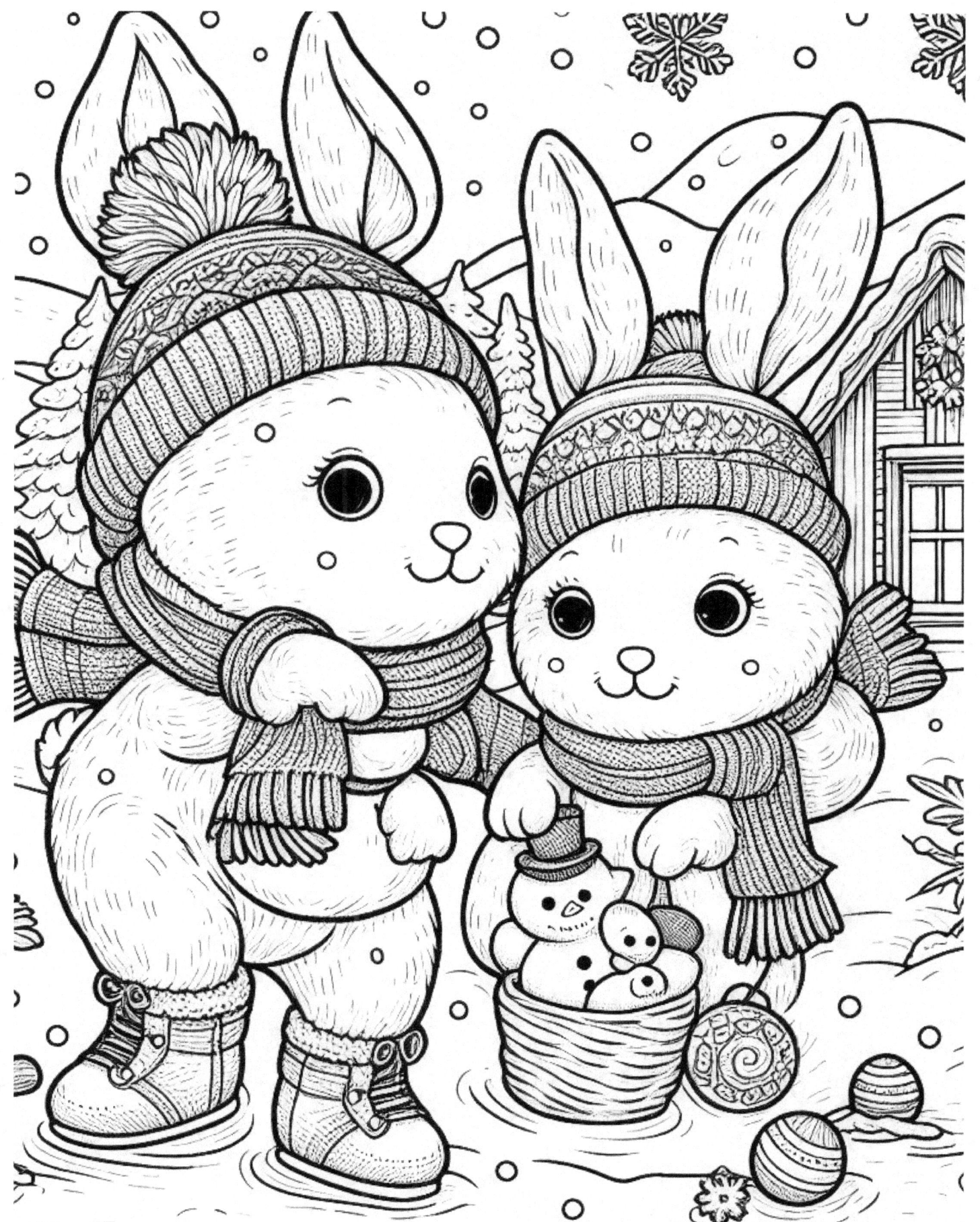

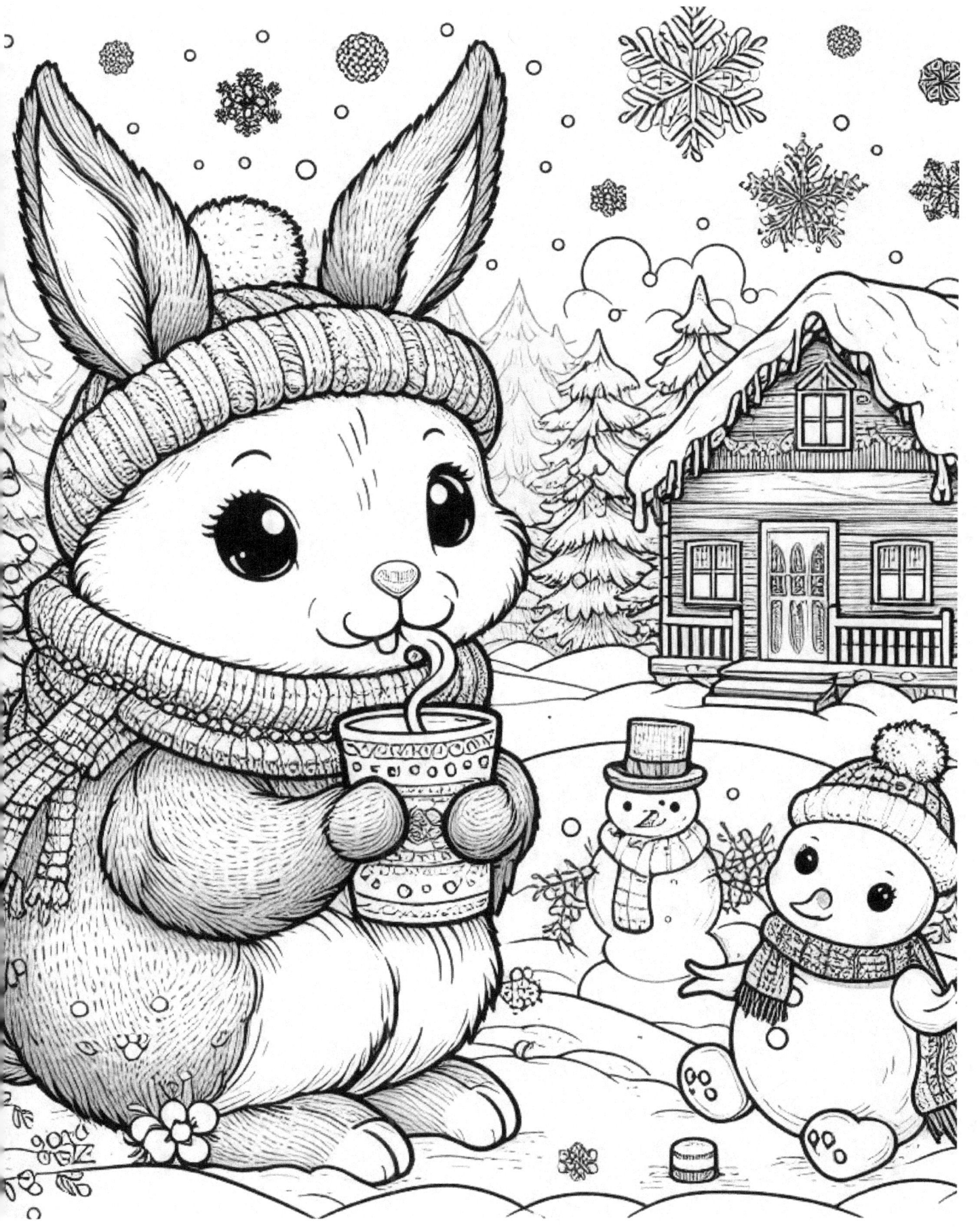

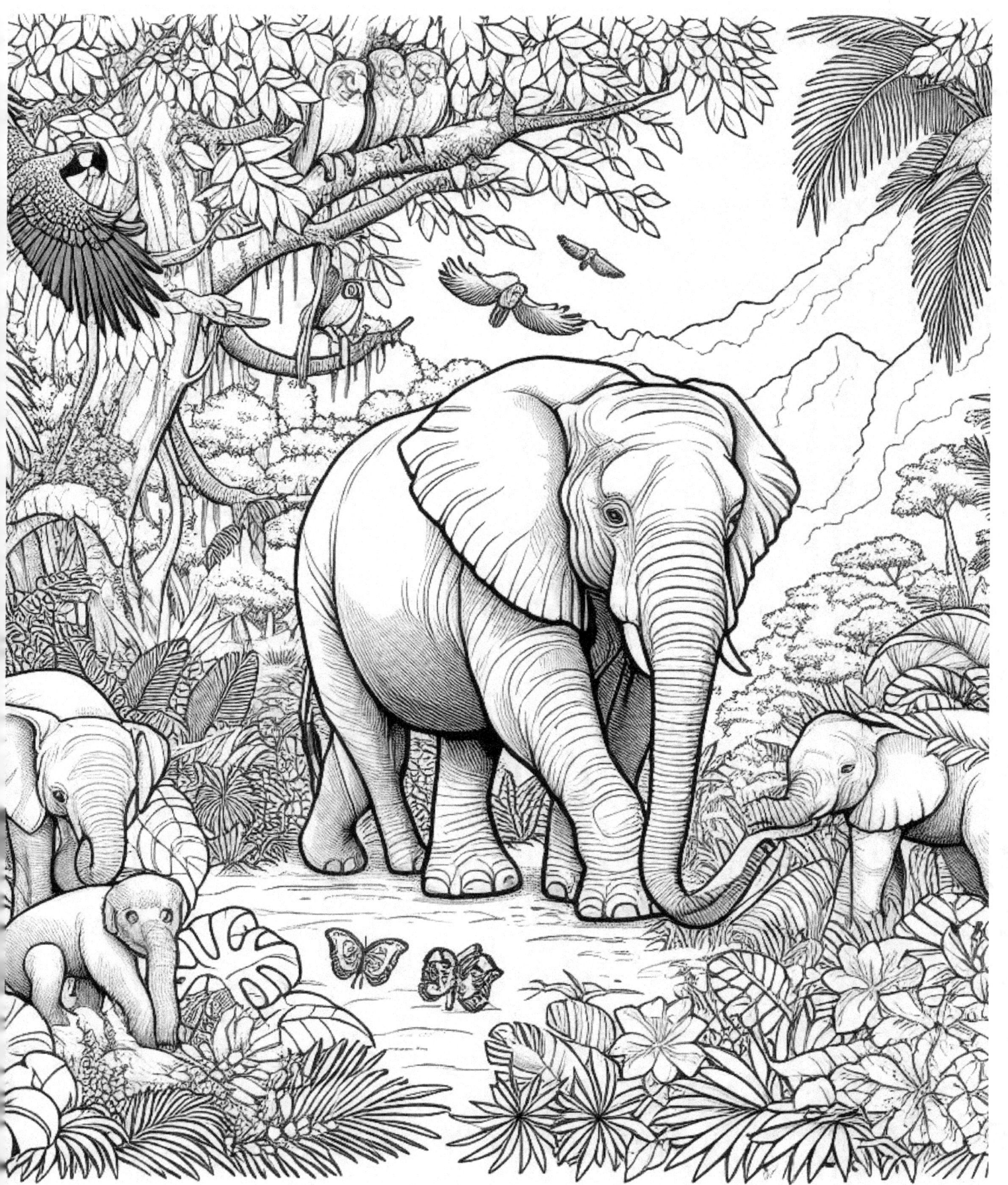

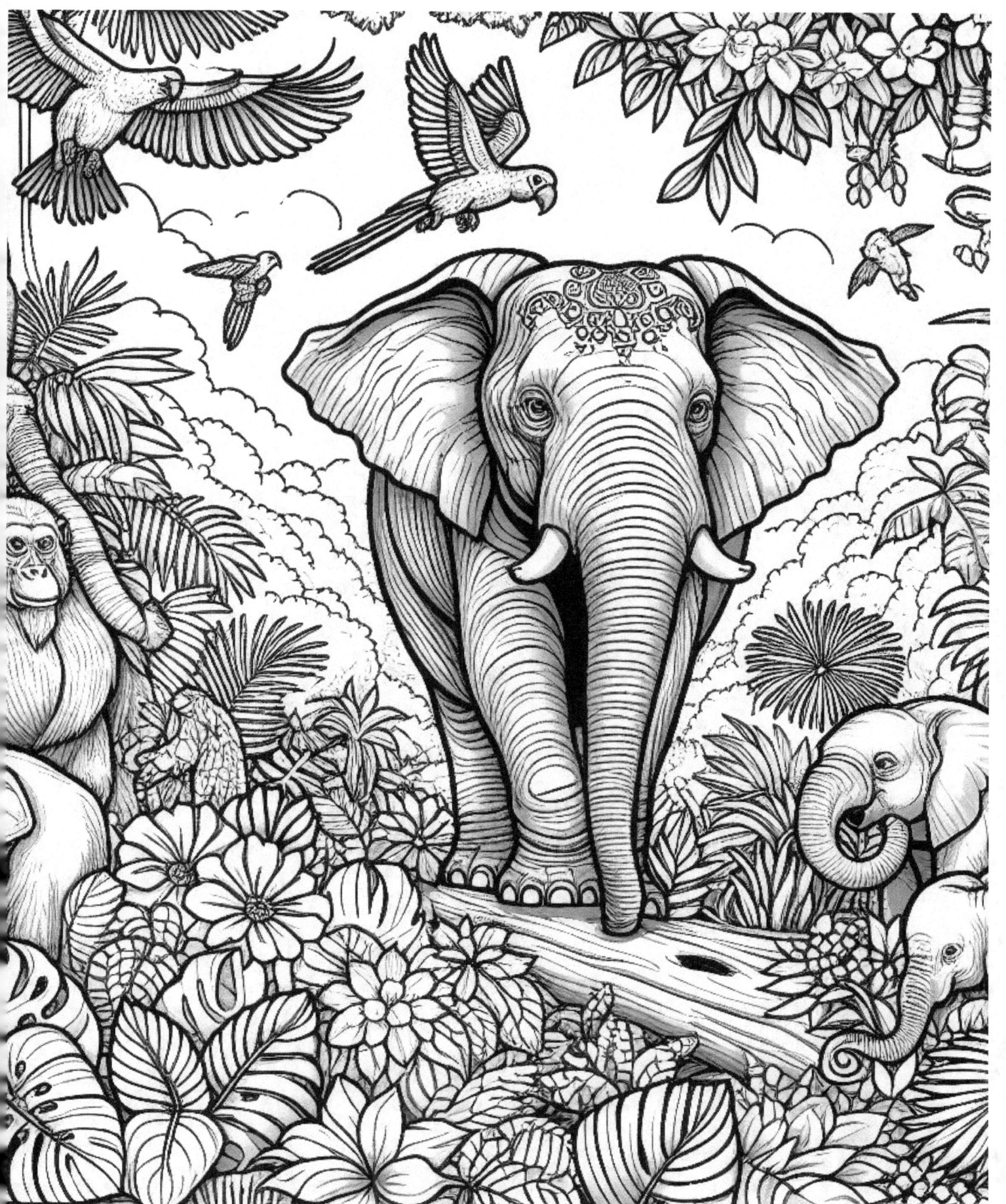

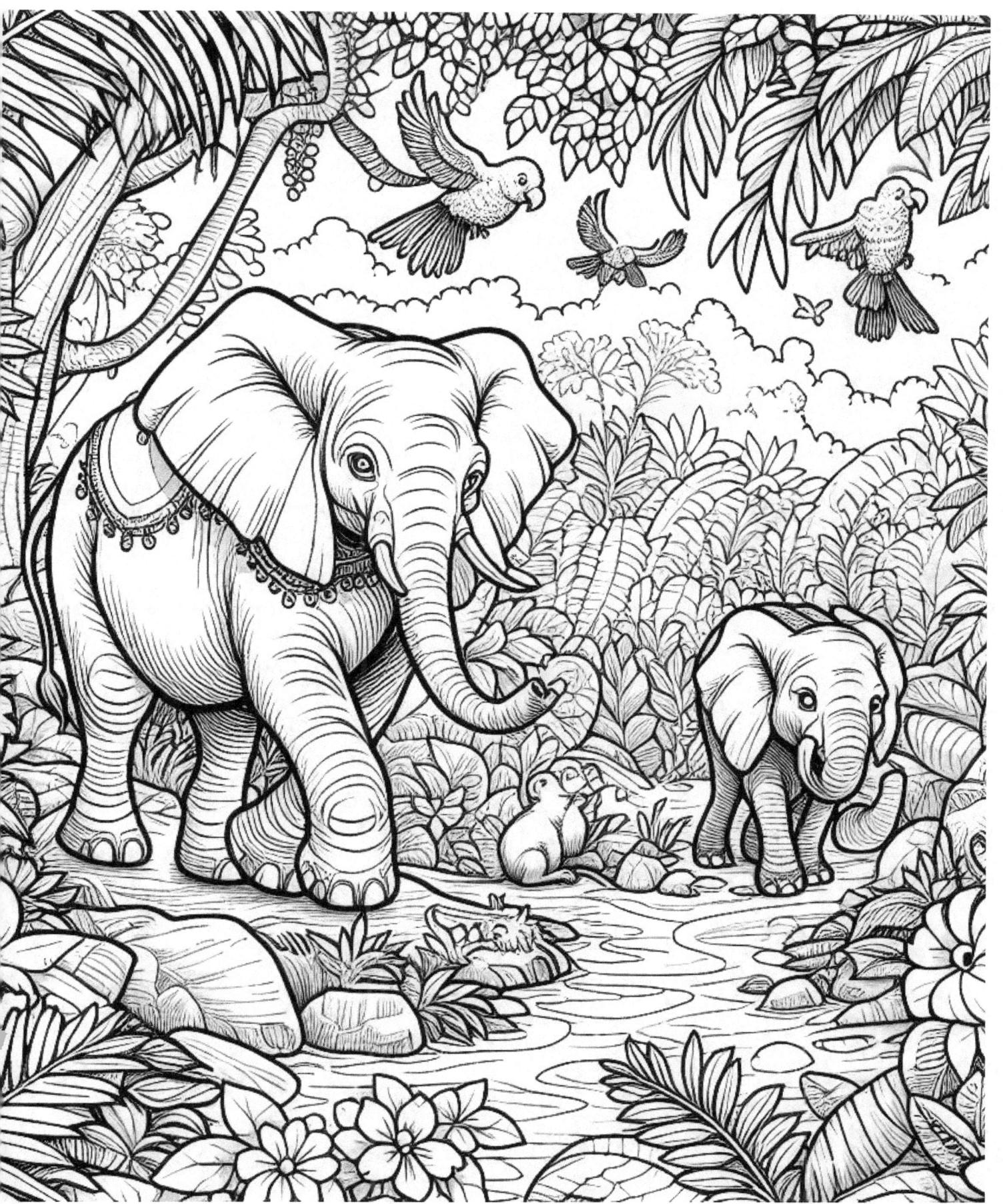

www.ingramcontent.com/pod-product-compliance
Lightning Source LLC
Chambersburg PA
CBHW082210220526
45470CB00010B/3112